Praise for   ☜ **W9-CDZ-260**

SHORT NATURE WALKS
ON LONG ISLAND

"If running isn't for you, maybe walking is! Short [Nature] Walks on Long Island is a classic in the field of local discovery by foot."
—Library News, Port Washington, NY

"With the hustle and bustle of confused compounded city life, one should 'come back to nature,' to recapture a oneness with land, sea, and stars. What better way than by walking."
—The New York Culture Review

" . . . directions, narrative and maps for memorable strolls and hikes."
—Northeast Outdoors

"Long Island is ready to tell you where the walking is great. Short [Nature] Walks on Long Island . . . is a series of interesting walking tours . . . that require anywhere from a half hour to two hours or more. But there's no hurry, and you can proceed at your own leisurely pace. Happy hiking."
—Newsday, Long Island, NY

"Rodney and Priscilla Albright explain, We know the hidden Long Island, which includes thousands of acres of woodland, wetland, beach, and estuary, because we have explored much of it on foot.' "
—New York Alive magazine

"The authors describe 52 short walks with travel directions and maps."
—F.Y.I. Travel Tips, Copley News Service

SHORT NATURE WALKS ON LONG ISLAND

Third Edition

by

Rodney and Priscilla Albright

CHESTER, CONNECTICUT

Library of Congress Cataloging-in-Publication Data

Albright, Rodney.
  Short Nature Walks on Long Island.

  1. Hiking—New York (State)—Long Island—Guide-books.
2. Long Island (New York)—Description and travel—
Guide-books.   I. Title.
GV199.42.N652L663   1988   917.47'210443   88-24390
ISBN 0-87106-675-0

Manufactured in the United States of America
Third Edition/Second Printing

Contents

Location of Short Walks on Long Island

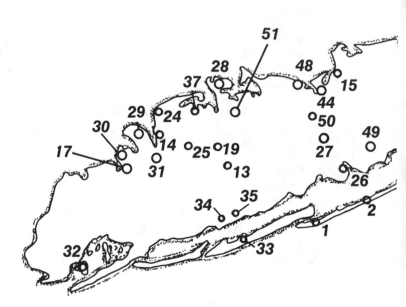

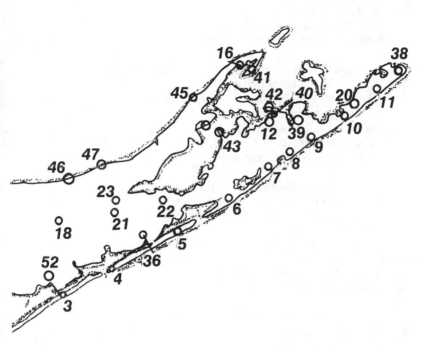

Salt Marshes and Fresh Water Creeks

Sand Spits and Points

North Shore Beaches

Preserves

On a fine May morning, quite early, we drove along Dune Road east of Quogue. There was no wind, and the pools of water in the salt marshes were just catching the beginning rays of the rising sun. We were not then birders to any serious degree, although we carried a pair of binoculars in the car. That morning we noticed a black and white sort of harlequin-looking bird at the edge of one of the pools. We took a good look at him, and later, referring to a bird guidebook, we realized we had seen a black-bellied plover in his spring plumage. This small discovery got us started really using our eyes, and it made us realize, too, that the birds still sought out the natural places on Long Island and maybe we should, too.

So we began walking in as many of the quiet places as we could seek out. In addition to being conscious of the fine air and the feeling of well-being, we began to make notes of the birds and the wildflowers in their seasons. We started compiling the good memories from each walk, and we went every week and the year round in search of the semblances of the original Long Island that are still there.

We found beautiful old woods in both Nassau and Suffolk counties, even though the harvesting of firewood for New York City took a great toll on the trees back in the eighteenth and early nineteenth centuries. When the railroad first came through, sparks from the coal-fired engines set some bad fires along the line.

The wetlands and estuaries and the grand sweep of the beaches reveal the great variety of natural beauty that has escaped the pressures of urban sprawl, the places where the glossy ibis feeds in the salt marshes, where the beach plum covers the dunes with her spring blossoms and the woodcock starts up from the cattails.

Contrary to our expectations, we have found that these open places in their natural states and available to the walker have actually increased in acreage during the past twenty years that we have watched Long Island closely. Conservationists working in towns, counties, state, and nation, in park departments, fish and wildlife services, and the Nature Conservancy have been alert for ecologically and biologically significant tracts of land that might be acquired and held for public use. These same agencies offer schools programs to make children aware of the fascinations that abound here and of the respect we must show this fragile heritage. This new edition of *Short Nature Walks on Long Island* is not intended as a complete trail guide to every possibility, but rather a selection of special places that we can attest to. We have made changes in the descriptions of walks, not physical changes but changes in the directions for getting there and in admissions fees, where applicable. We have added a few new places that seemed especially accessible and pleasant. And, incidentally, we know now that the aforementioned black-bellied plover, far from being "rare," is a regular visitor to Long Island, where you are bound to see him if you keep on looking!

Walking on Long Island

Walking on Long Island takes you into bracing air, clears your mind, and sharpens your senses. It's refreshing. You don't have to scramble up hillsides or over rocks. There is no need for blazes or fear of getting lost, and the only equipment needed is comfortable clothing and reasonably stout shoes. Of course, the birder mustn't fail to bring his binoculars nor the photographer her camera for there are abundant opportunities to use that kind of equipment.

Considering the proximity of Long Island to the city there are still many places where Nature has held her own and, when man has cooperated, has prospered. We've walked here for years and recommend it. Here are some suggestions:

Most of these places are most satisfactorily explored by two or three people, not groups. Due to extreme pressures of population, many of the towns with beaches limit access at the peak of the season to residents with permits; and other restrictions pertain to the county parks. Walkers, however, are usually accommodated. It's usually the cars that are the problem. So be attentive, quiet, and courteous—and don't litter.

If these admonitions seem gratuitous—and indeed they might, with all the messages we receive today about litter and pollution— you will understand our deep concern as you take a closer look at our world. For as you move about on foot, you'll be constantly aware of both the fragility and the brave tenacity of nature. And because of the enjoyment you'll get from it, you'll want to admonish others to take care, too.

A word about hazards that aren't very frightening but should be noted in passing. Have an eye out for posion ivy, which pops up almost anywhere, and ticks have received a lot of publicity because of Lyme disease. They are present in the vegetation, usually in high grass. Do check for those tiny devils when you get home. Follow regular rules of behavior in case of an electrical storm and wear a hat to fend off sunstroke!

This book, we hope, will give you seasonal choices for walks. Perhaps in the height of summer you'll want to seek out the wooded, cooler places and walk the beaches when the swimmers have gone home, although if you're willing to get out early and walk away from the life-guarded areas, you'll soon be out of the beach crowds. The towns will most certainly be more appealing when the crowds have thinned.

But the fact is taking a walk is almost always a good thing to do. If it's drizzling and overcast, it's a good day to walk; if it's cold or windy—or cold *and* windy—it's a good day to walk. Just dress appropriately. As Henry David Thoreau wrote, "When we walk, we naturally go to the fields and woods: what would become of us, if we walked only in a garden or a mall?"

Long Island, viewed only from its parkways, might appear to be a vast sprawl of elegant shopping centers, discreet industrial parks, and housing developments in all styles of achitecture. But we know another, hidden Long Island, which includes thousands of acres of woodland, wetland, beach, and estuary, because we have explored much of it on foot.

Contrary to our expectations we find that these open places in their natural states have actually increased in acreage during the past dozen or more years we have watched Long Island closely. Conservationists working in towns, counties, state, and nation, in park departments, fish and wildlife service, and The Nature Conservancy have been alert for ecologically and biologically significant tracts of land that might be acquired and held for public use. These same agencies offer the schools programs to make children aware of the fascinations that abound here and of the respect we must show this fragile heritage.

It is our intent in this little book to introduce you to a wide range of these places, secluded places—urban wilds is an expression we have heard, and a good description of what we have looked for. We are interested in the relaxation that comes easily with getting out-of-doors and striding down some quiet path. It soothes away the tensions and stresses of our busy, noisy, crowded-together world. We like to drive away from these conditions as often as we can and to park someplace to get off alone, or relatively so, to observe the world in its natural state.

This new edition of *Short Walks on Long Island* is not intended as a complete trail guide to every possibility, but rather a selection of special places that we can attest to from one end of the island to the other. We have made changes in many of the walks, not physical changes for the most part, but changes in the directions for getting there and in admission fees, where applicable. And we have added a number of new places because, thanks to the conservationists mentioned above, land has been acquired and public entry made possible in numerous places we could not walk when the book was first printed.

SHORT NATURE WALKS
ON LONG ISLAND

Robert Moses State Park is the westernmost 1,000 acres of Fire Island and is reachable by car across causeway and bridge, which take you over Great South Bay and Fire Island Inlet to several parking fields accommodating more than 5,000 cars. It is parkway all 49 miles from New York City.

Since this broad flat beach is walkable any time of year, you will never be alone hiking. It is something of an adventure, because its ready accessibility draws a wide assortment of people attracted here by the sea, the sand, the spaciousness of its open sky. But it is refreshing. Breathing air tempered by the sea, observing others reveling in the out-of-doors, and watching the sandpipers scurrying to surf's edge but wheeling away into the air as you approach, always keeping a distance from you, you'll discover somehow time will pass more quickly than you'd imagine. So look at your watch as you leave the parking area. There is uninterrupted beach ahead for 31 miles. More than you can walk today.

From the easternmost large parking lot (labeled field 5) the distances are:

East to the Lighthouse 1.4 miles

East to Kismet (first Fire Island community) 2.1 miles

East to the Sunken Forest 6.7 miles

West to Lookout Tower at Fire Island Inlet 3.4 miles

The beach, known for many years as Great South Beach, is indeed great, one of the finest beaches in the world. As you visit at different

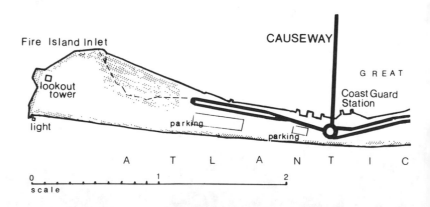

seasons, you will see that it changes size and shape, is cut away in winter, flattens out in summer. Erosion brings change, as does the longshore transport of sand by currents. The lighthouse, which was built in 1856, replaced the first one built at the western tip of the island in 1825. It is now 5 miles inland. But the Corps of Engineers keeps dredging out the ship channel that separates it from the next island to the west so Fire Island no longer actively grows westward.

For a short walk head out eastward. We clock ourselves, going for about an hour, then turn around and come back, and advise you to do the same. You will probably get to the lighthouse or a bit beyond.

Perhaps it is best, if you seek solitude, to walk here after a storm or during the rain when most people will not venture afield. But people flock together, and groups thin out as you go eastward.

There are refreshment stands, picnic shelters, and a bathhouse open in season.

ROBERT MOSES STATE PARK

To reach Sailor's Haven, take the ferry from Sayville. Ferries operate on regular schedules from May to November. If you can arrange it and have the stamina, you can get a ferry at Patchogue to Davis Park, then walk along the beach westward to Sailor's Haven, a distance of 5.7 miles, returning by ferry to Sayville.*

The waves of the great Atlantic Ocean, set in motion 600 or more miles offshore by the wind, head westward unimpeded, slide up over the continental shelf, and, with almost hourly changes of mood, strike the Long Island south shore beaches with pulsations of fascinating and hypnotic qualities. Its visual aspects change too, so frequently in fact that there is never a dull day at the beach. There is never the threat of oppressive crowds. It is glorious. There is a fascination that nothing can quite describe, drawing you back again and again, refreshing you—and quietly luring you into spending an hour or a day longer than you had in mind.

We have come in the early spring, starting off in weather so thick we could not see Fire Island from the Sayville side, to have the sun later break through to show off the carpet of beach heather climbing these dunes, golden in bloom.

As the barrier beach built up, collecting more and more sand, the wind piled it up and formed these dunes. While some are only 4 or 5 feet high, many, as these here, reach a height of 35 or 40 feet.

*Watch Hill and Davis Park ferry: (516) 475-1665; Sailor's Haven (Sunken Forest) ferry: (516) 589-8980. Another alternative would be to take the ferry from the seashore terminal at the head of the Patchogue River over to Watch Hill. From there Sailor's Haven would be a walk of 6.6 miles.

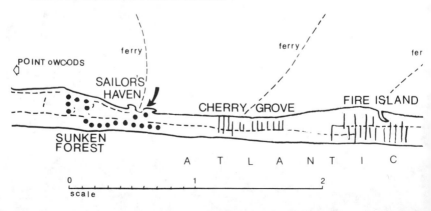

Behind the dunes, between Cherry Grove and Point O'Woods, is a sanctuary well worth a visit that affords a pleasant walk. The Sunken Forest has pretty close to 600 feet of frontage on the beach and comprises almost 40 acres of land. It is a short walk, close to the Sailor's Haven ferry dock. As you cross to the south and climb the ramps protecting the dunes, you rise 35 feet above sea level and look across the top of the dunes to the Great South Bay beyond.

The dense vegetation between you and the bay is the top of the forest. Now rare, although there have been many similar forests in New Jersey as well as Cape Cod, the Sunken Forest of Fire Island has fortunately been preserved, and we are able to see here many trees that are estimated to be a hundred years old. The principal trees are holly, tupelo, and sassafras, grown to a height of 35 to 40 feet. Normally these species do not reach this size because they are crowded out by stronger, taller growing trees. Here, however, the red maple, red cedar, black and post oak, and pitch pine are themselves sheared off by the winds from the ocean and thus are stunted to the protecting screen height of the dunes. It is dense with the tangles of wild grape, catbrier, a floor of ferns, Canada mayflower, and false Solomon's seal.

Descending the path into this primitive forest, you have an unusual experience similar to being in a jungle and interesting too because of the land birds. The boardwalk comes out on the bay side into almost blinding light if it is a bright day, through thickets of plume grass, hugs the sandy shore, and reenters the forest to the west, twining back through the area. On a hot summer day it's pleasantly cool.

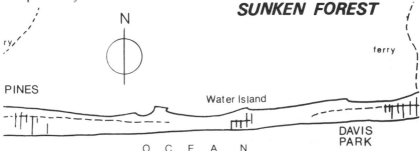

The beach accessible at Smith Point West is one of our favorite places to walk, and the 7-mile stretch westward to Watch Hill is presently the only "National Wilderness" in New York State—only recently so established and consequently not open to vehicles. A causeway and bridge lead to the eastern end of the island, where there's ample parking (parking fee in summer months). This is at the south end of the William Floyd Parkway. Train service on the Montauk line goes to Shirley Station, 2.5 miles from the bridge.

A two-story octagonal visitor center on the dunes houses the National Seashore ranger's office, which is open year round and contains an informative display on beach life. Rangers guide interesting short walks from here in the summer.

The beach westward offers a walk stretchable as far as you'll be able to go. We usually head for the Old Inlet, which is a little more than 2 miles. The National Seashore maintains a shower-restroom building there during the summer and an ocean-to-bay boardwalk as well as a small dock with a buoy-marked channel leading to it. In moderate or cold weather it's nice to come back on the sand trail that runs inland parallel to the ocean.

At low tide pebbles are exposed which, in their wet state, may get you started on a pebble collection! There are white ones and black, red ones and brown, lavender, and with subtle variations, a seemingly limitless selection. In fact, that's where all the sand comes from, from the rocks and stones beating against each other, reducing

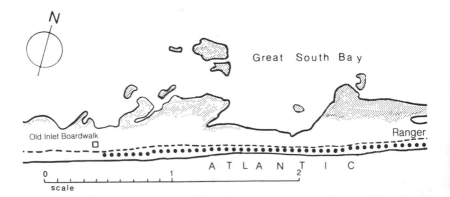

themselves into smaller and smaller pieces, sand being the smallest particles to which they are ever reduced. Scoop up these dry sands and, as they run through your fingers, investigate them carefully. At least half the sand is quartz, but there is hornblende, rutile, feldspar, augite, magnetite, ilmenite—a variety of names to confound you or just possibly to start you exploring a whole new world of minerals and rock. Below Hatteras, down into the beaches of the south, much of the sand is made up of tiny shell fragments, but not here on Long Island. Shells are relatively scarce. The rocks that make up these beaches were brought by the mighty glaciers of the ice age all the way from Canada. So as you inspect the debris of the sand you might find anything. They tell me specks of ruby and emerald exist here—but rarely! However, if you search, you'll certainly find garnet, and the black patches contain magnetite, an important ore sometimes possessing polarity, when it does, called lodestone. If you run a magnet through this, you'll find particles will cling.

With no people living on this thin stretch of the barrier beach, a walk here exposes some of the fragile links in the chain of life. For among the variety of life zones—the tidal edge of the sea, the beach itself, behind the sandy swales of the dunes, and in the wetlands along the Great South Bay—is a busy world to capture your interest and excite your imagination. We see hoof prints of deer here often, but deer are remarkable in becoming invisible. Only once or twice have we actually seen them here, and then what a thrill!

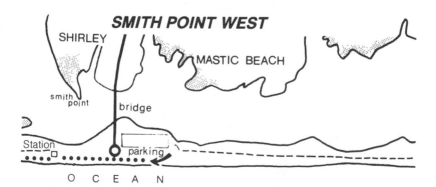

Now, since almost the entire stretch is privately owned, access to the beaches is limited if you have no local connections. The western tip at Moriches, however, is county owned, and although the parking area maintained there is limited to Suffolk County residents in summer months, we have frequently walked here off season.

To reach this western tip, you drive south from the Montauk Highway on Mill Road, and at the second stop light, you turn right onto Potunk Lane, soon passing a very handsome church on the left. Then follow Jessup Lane across the bridge and turn right on Dune Road. Thence it is 4.5 miles west to the end of the road. From here along the edge of the ocean the distance to the jetty at Moriches Inlet is 1.5 miles. The surf can be formidable, crashing and spuming; there has been some geysering here on a couple of occasions when we've walked! Because the point is without habitations, it can be marvelously wild. We turn north at the jetty and walk back along the inlet to the quieter waters on Moriches Bay. Offshore the islands are breeding areas for skimmers and terns, and you should be stealthy and alert for this is an especially good birding spot for larger shore birds and wanderers. The sand is firm, and you'll find secluded pockets to stretch out to relax if you wish. Then, after continuing northeastward for a quarter of a mile, you'll find a road leading up from the water to the center of the dunes and to another road paralleling the ocean, which will bring you back to the parking lot. These grassy dunes are spacious and filled with interdune plant

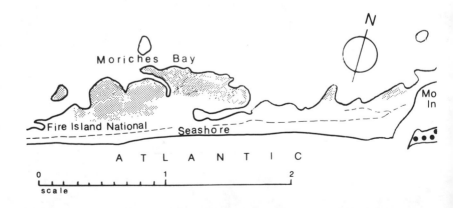

and wildlife. In the summer months they can be too hot for comfort, but out of season they are magnificent, and late in the day, the low light gives them the Elvira Madigan look, which is so romantic.

In September 1938 when the hurricane hit this beach, it had not been anticipated. Thunderstorms occurred the night before, but next morning everyone set about his business as usual. Heavy rain didn't start until 1:00 P.M., and winds reached 45 mph. By 3:00 P.M. the situation became critical, a gale was howling, and water was all over the beach. The center of the storm hit Westhampton before other places to the east. The tide was 10 to 15 feet above normal, and the sea beat at and broke through the dunes. Only the higher ones or stronger bulkheads held. New inlets were cut through into Quantuck and Shinnecock bays. From Mecox to Sagaponack Pond, the ocean broke through at five places!

WESTHAMPTON BEACH

Cross the bridge at Quogue or Hampton Bays on to Dune Road. About midway between the two is Tiana Beach, where there's parking and easy access across the dunes.

Wide and open, the beach here is strung out with cottages all along behind the dunes, but not dominating the landscape. We generally walk a mile west, by the round apartment complex and several summer places to the Quogue Public Beach, and return. Then we walk another mile east to total an hour and a half or two hours of elapsed time. It is never too crowded.

Low tide is the best time to walk on the beach because the wet sand is compacted and settled by the waves, so all along the water's edge the firm walkway is hard enough not to hold you back in your own footsteps. Actually, water still remains between the individual grains of sand, and even on the hottest days the sun only dries the surface. There's a microscopic world of channels and ponds teeming with almost invisible life. Just watch the tiny sandpipers scurrying up to the water's edge, pecking away into the oozing sand. That's what they're after.

Quite apart from our walks, however, another reason compels us to come back here. That is Dune Road. The variety of shore birds using the wetlands along the north of the road is almost endless. Almost all these creatures who nest or visit Long Island can be seen at some spot along here, wading in the shallows, standing in the grass, or winging low over the water. During the migratory season

you will see one or two dunlin, black-bellied plover, ruddy turn-stone, and then another and another, until you realize that the grass or shoreline is alive with them.

Come equipped with glasses and your bird guide. You'll find your car a perfect blind from which to observe. Drive along slowly. We've seen and heard the clapper rail with his raucous call and watched the bittern slowly swaying as he holds his bill in the air pretending to be a reed, trying to elude us. And we have watched black skimmer after black skimmer feeding, with their precision glide along the water. You'll see it all on Dune Road.

The slimy wetlands swarm with insects, and the water is unfit to drink. But acre for acre, the salt marsh will produce more plants than any farm, fertilizing itself, needing no help from man in plant-ing or harvesting. Not only is it the feeding grounds for migrating birds you see along Dune Road, but it provides shelter and food for small mammals as well. We've watched the muskrat swimming here and working in the shallows, for example. And the tiny fish that swim and breed here are carried out on tides to feed still larger fish miles from shore. When you see the fill on some of this wetland, you realize that environmentalists do not always win the continuing battle with developers.

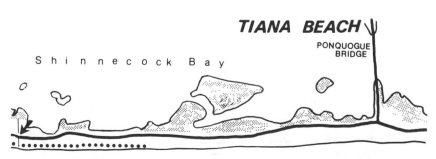

TIANA BEACH

PONQUOGUE
BRIDGE

Shinnecock Bay

OCEAN

From the Shinnecock Inlet in Southampton eastward, the beach stretches in a broad unbroken swath for 11 miles to Sagaponack Pond. In summer this area attracts, for the most part, those who are content to lie out in the sun, dip in the magnificent surf—sometimes it's too magnificent and must be respected—and picnic or fling the frisbee. Off season it is almost completely uninhabited except for the occasional dog walker, surf fisherman, or bird watcher.

There are many places of public access where you may park. Sometimes there is a fee or a parking permit is required (obtained either at the Southampton Village or one of the two town halls or at the beach). Out of season, however, there is no problem.

This stretch is characterized by high dunes; rather large summer houses, set usually well behind the dunes for protection; a number of guarded beaches for swimming; good walking at low tide; and many ponds just behind the dunes where there is always more to be seen than a bird. At the east end of Shinnecock Bay the beach ceases to be a barrier island (or here a peninsula) and all the rest of the way to Montauk becomes part of the mainland. These are classic beaches, the kind you see in marvelous color prints, the dunes covered with pale chartreuse grasses and over the broad stretches of white sand, a mist of salt spray, the sun catching the movement of the waves.

At the Shinnecock or western end of this stretch there are no buildings at all, and the dunes are unusually high. Terns must nest

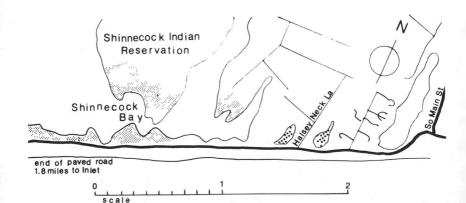

Shinnecock Indian Reservation

Shinnecock Bay

Halsey Neck La

So Main St

N

end of paved road
1.8 miles to Inlet

0   1   2

scale

here, for once in the spring they literally dive-bombed us. Parking out here is informal. The road peters out, so be careful unless you have a four-wheel-drive vehicle. The walk to the jetty is about 2 miles.

There are three or four other accesses to the beach. Our favorite section to walk is the one locally known as Fowlers. The approach to the high dunes is through broad potato fields, some seasons planted to wheat for rotation. The parking is along one side of the lane, so your walk is first to get to the beach, looking for wild things near the ponds. On both sides they usually have interesting birds. And in August they are surrounded by huge pink or rose flowers of the marsh mallow. We turn left as we come onto the beach, walk along the water to Mecox Bay and back, making a total distance of just over 3 miles. This is a comfortable walk for us and includes the goal of getting to the big bay to watch sailboats or see if we can spot a long-billed dowitcher lurking in the shallows. The surfing must be pretty good for there is always a young crowd there complete with boards and wet suits. And, incidentally, in winter there is ice boating on Mecox Bay.

Beach walks clear your mind of many things. Often personal problems are replaced by other thoughts such as those stemming from the fact that geologists say these beaches are a million years old!

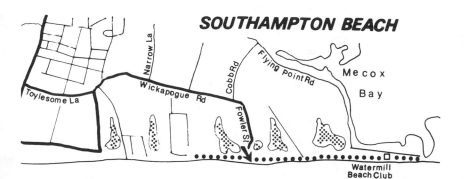

SOUTHAMPTON BEACH

Of the five unbroken stretches of beach along Long Island's south shore, Wainscott Beach, 3.6 miles from end to end, is the shortest. Many walkers have a compulsion to cover every mile of a stretch, just because it is there, and it's easy to understand the urge because there is a satisfaction to having traversed any stretch. Still, on the broad flat strands of the coastline here, there isn't a startling surprise of discovery. One beach is very much like another. There are differences, of course, but these differences are subtle, sometimes more metaphysical than real. And since, from hour to hour, aspects of the beach walking experience change anyway, it can be misleading to describe any of Long Island's beaches in specific detail. Wainscott Beach is probably the most out of the way. There are cottages all along, well back in grassy stretches. The dunes are lower. For some reason driftwood does not accumulate here to the extent it does farther east. Freighters at sea seem farther out.

To reach Wainscott Beach, turn south from the Montauk Highway 1.3 miles west of Bridgehampton on Main Street to Sagaponack, and on to the end; or to the end of Beach Lane in Wainscott.

It's a good idea to check the tide tables before you start off and try to do your principal walking during the low tide, when the footing is more solid and the walking easier! Up on the higher ground the surface sand does dry to a greater depth and walking becomes more laborious.

When you stand on the beach facing the sea, you can notice from many little indicators that the water pulls to the west. For the longest time we simply couldn't understand this. We'd say that the Gulf Stream was out there moving eastward and northward along the coast, so how could the water here along shore move as it obviously does, in the opposite direction? Have you asked yourself this question? Have you seen how the sand moves with the currents west, how pieces of driftwood move back toward New York? In a word, the answer is friction. The Gulf Stream is a very large river, about 40 miles wide and 2,000 feet deep, with a volume of water a thousand times larger than our biggest river, and it moves about 5.5 miles per hour in a northeasterly direction. As it moves, the water along the shore is set into currents and eddies that flow for a time in the reverse direction because of the friction of the shore.

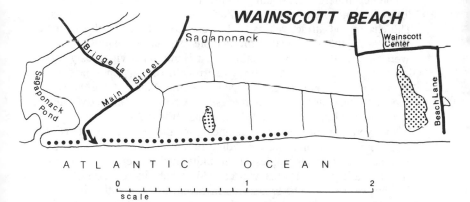

From Georgica Pond the Long Island South Beach is uninterrupted for 22.2 miles to Montauk. Locally the stretch is referred to
as East Hampton Beach, Amagansett Beach, Napeague Beach, or
Montauk Beach, depending on its proximity to the adjoining community. The entire stretch is magnificent and eminently walkable.

Parking on East Hampton beaches is restricted to residents only
during the season. East Hampton is chic, as a town, beautifully
maintained, handsome because of tree-shaded lanes and many attractive houses. It has a casual dignity and considerable local civic
pride. We've driven along streets here early in the morning, before
breakfast, on the way to the beach and seen golden pheasant, one
after another, strutting across village greenswards. This pastoral,
relaxed village atmosphere is the secret of East Hampton's jealously
guarded charm, and a strong effort is being made to keep it this way.

A good walk on the East Hampton Beach is from the village beach
east of Hook Pond; walk westward to the Georgica Pond inlet and
return. The total distance, round-trip, is 6.4 miles. On your right as
you head out will be the Maidstone Golf Club and Hook Pond,
which is a good birding area. Beyond Main Street Beach the dune
area is fairly primitive, low and windswept. Off season you can find
a place to park.

The beach here is in striking contrast to, say, the beaches west of
Jones Beach, where our urban sprawl has crowded out the dunes.
The charm and attractiveness of Eastern Long Island is threatened
by growth—the statistically predictable population explosion and
overcrowding that seem inevitable. East Hampton is vigorously trying to preserve its heritage, limit its growth, save its open land for
living space. The East End Chapter of the Nature Conservancy,
known as the South Fork–Shelter Island Chapter, is an active one.
Acres of land have been saved through its efforts. As you walk Long
Island, you will appreciate its openness, see the need to save its wild
areas, but feel the pressures crowding in to crush its rural character.
You may feel yourself helpless as an individual in a crowded society
and may ask yourself what you can do to help in conserving this.
The answer seems to be to become involved, to work with others for
a common end. The administration of our civic affairs apparently
works under pressure of an aroused citizenry. The South Fork–
Shelter Island Chapter is located in Amagansett, where acquisition,
education, and public information are coordinated.

EAST HAMPTON BEACH

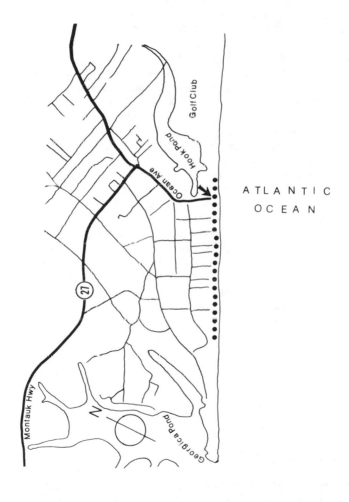

0   1   2
Scale

An easy direct access to Amagansett Beach is to turn south off the Montauk Highway on Indian Wells Highway (just out of East Hampton but before you reach Amagansett). At its end is a bathhouse on the east side, and opposite this, Sheppard's Dunes, an eight-acre area acquired and protected by the Nature Conservancy to preserve its natural state. Parking during the season is reserved for residents. It's better to walk in late spring or early fall anyway.

The beach itself has character. Houses sit almost half a mile up from the beach on bluffs overlooking the sea, and the dunes are wild. So our suggestion is to walk to Maidstone Golf Club, which is 2.5 miles to the west on the wide beach, then return.

For anyone who has lived in inland wooded areas, the plants and ground cover of the seashore offer a fascinating world of discovery. When there's a break in the dunes, as there is here, you can be tempted to cross in order to examine interior plant life. But don't do it. You will crush the dune grasses, make the passage vulnerable to wind erosion. And just one such spot can actually weaken an entire dune. So be conservation minded and alert to damage to any plant life. You will be able to find a path allowing you to observe.

The beach grass, with its long curving leaves, is the principal stabilizer for the dunes. It gets its nourishment from wind-blown minerals, grows up, sends its roots deep, follows the contours of the dunes. The false heather is another, with bright buttery yellow blossoms from May through July. It is a low shrubby plant adapted to life on the shifting sands.

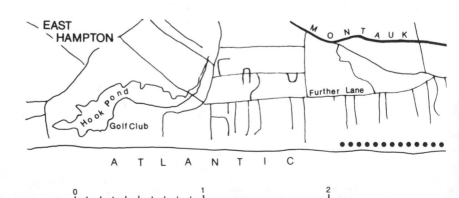

Just over the dunes, when there's soil enough, the beach pea will take hold, send its vinelike leaflets swarming, the ends with little tendrils like a pig's tail. You will want to examine the pea flowers which are delicate in shades of violet and purple, blossoming throughout the summer. Inland, thickets of beach plum and bayberry take hold with beautiful fruit in the fall.

When the dunes are stabilized, it is amazing the exuberance that nature displays. Above all, you should beware the poison ivy, rampant near the beach. You will find rugosa rose, seaside goldenrod, thistle, and blueberry. It is really quite startling to realize the wide variety there is in plant life near the beach.

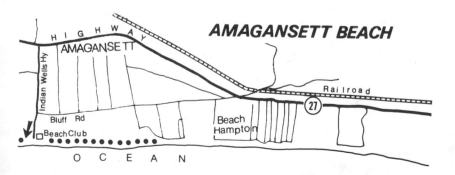

After you leave Amagansett, driving east, the ocean comes into view from the highway for the first time. The peninsula abruptly narrows; two bodies of water—Napeague Bay and Harbor—extend southward, making the land here less than a mile wide until you reach Hither Hills (about 6 miles). The road parallels the ocean about a half mile inland. The land is flat with low dunes and familiar seaside plants. Napeague Beach extends eastward from Amagansett. It's easiest to get onto the beach through the Hither Hills State Park.

Out here is a good place to get a feeling for the forces that shaped Long Island's topographical features. As you leave, you see Amagansett, the high dunes petering out, then at Hither Hills the land mass piles up again, now in contours and hills that are more than 150 feet above sea level here. The land masses are the result of the swath pushed and dumped here by the glaciers, and the beaches, from the continuous action, ever since, of wind and sea. Great rolling breakers have been moving in on the Long Island shoreline for a million years since the first glacier came down, and for more than 25,000 years since the last, scooping up rocks and sand, rubbing and grinding and depositing the fine, fine particles, forming the present continuous beach. And wind has blown it around. What with storms and tides and longshore transit of sands by currents, there have been constant changes in elevations and shorelines. It is recorded that there were seven inlets east of Fire Island in 1743—but then Fire Island was 55 miles long. It was not until 1931 that big

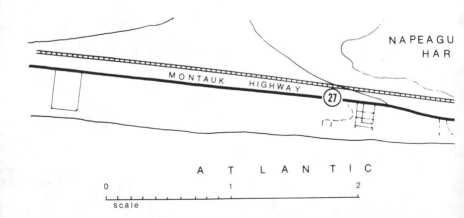

waves and high tides separated the dunes and broke through Fire Island at Moriches Inlet in a destructive storm. And it is inevitable that there will be further change.

As you walk the Napeague Beach, go east for a time and see the high bluffs where the southern moraine comes right to the sea. Turn around and walk past the park to the low dunes. Along the way you will surely see a fisherman or two.

An underwater sandbar extends almost the entire length of the island about a quarter mile offshore, formed by the undertow. And you will generally see commercial and sport fishing boats trolling along over this bar. The fishing is apt to be good. At least surf-casters have this attitude. During the summer there are schools of bluefish, sea bass, porgies, and flounder. Late in the autumn striped bass can be caught and, through the winter, cod.

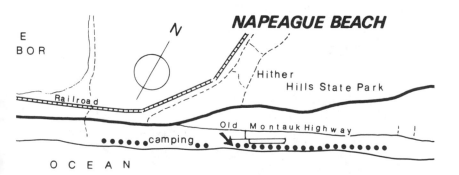

There's a gap in the morainal hills which is properly Montauk Beach, about a 3.5-mile stretch of broad sandy beach, from the high dunes along the Old Montauk Highway. East of this you come to the 70-foot-high bluffs, a kind of land's end, halfway between New York City and the farthest reach of Cape Cod, which is Montauk Point. There are places to park right in town and easy access. The beach is nice and wide. There will be bathers and people lying in the sun if it's summer. And if you walk west toward the dunes, you should surely see surfers in wet suits, because the conditions are evidently good there.

The kinds of waves on which surfboarders get the best ride are known as spilling breakers—or those which, as they approach the beach, have a line of foam spilling down their front, always just about to break but holding off for quite a while. Since the more gradual the slope of the bottom, the longer the wave will hold off breaking, it stands that the best surfing is on that kind of beach that has a long stretch underwater with almost no slope at all.

There is never a day on these waters when there is no surf whatsoever, though it is possible it can be too dull for those who make a sport of it. The whole science of waves is complex, but it is interesting to know that a wave will break when the ratio of the height of the wave to the depth of water is about three to four; that is to say that a 6-foot wave will break in about 8 feet of water.

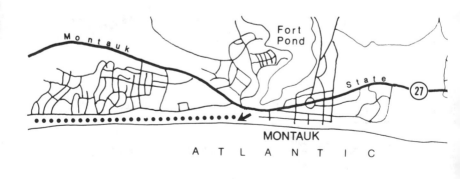

The wave action is caused principally by the wind's force against the surface of the water. The water itself actually moves very little. You can see this when you watch a cork or piece of driftwood bobbing at sea, and after the wave has passed, you see how little the cork has moved. When a wave passes through very shallow waters, it lifts and stirs up sand from the bottom, so the loose grains of sand settle in a place different from where it started. That's how waves change and shape the contours of beaches.

The changes in the beach would not, most likely, startle the Montauk Indians whose name it bears, and who were so naturally protected here from their mainland enemies, and who made quantities of wampum on these beaches from the shells of periwinkles and quahogs. No, these changes would not startle them half so much as the changes on land, where the indigenous hardwoods of New England—beech, oak, and maple—and of the 140- or 150-foot tulip trees from which they fashioned their canoes have all been destroyed.

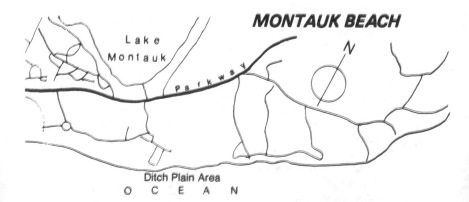

Towns To Do on Foot

One of the joys of walking is to step out of the fetters of time, to while away and unwind at a leisurely pace and with a certain detachment. Keeping alert to the surroundings in this carefree state, you'll experience a satisfaction. Walking along the edge of the sea may give you a sense of leaping back in time to first beginnings, and walking along narrow streets of an old village may make you feel nostalgic, feeding your hankering for a simpler life.

Long Island was colonized by New Englanders, mostly from Connecticut, and English architectural influences are visible in a number of places, some dating as far back as the Old House in Cutchogue. There are Dutch influences too which pushed eastward from New Amsterdam.

Rural village charms that still exist on Long Island are mainly left over from the nineteenth century. By then the settlement had established a character that has strong appeal to us today. Civic pride is responsible for considerable restoration in recent years. There are other communities you might want to explore besides the six little communities we describe here. They offer interesting architecture and still retain vestiges of rural village charms. We suggest you go out of your way to investigate *Amityville*, south of Farmingdale at the end of Broad Hollow Road and south of the Sunrise Highway; *Roslyn Park*, just south of the North Hempstead Turnpike between Port Washington Boulevard and Glen Cove Road; *Cold Spring Harbor*, on Harbor Road just north of North Hempstead Turnpike between Glen Cove and Huntington; and *Oyster Bay Village*, all in Nassau County. And in Suffolk County, visit *Northport*, east of Huntington and Centerport, north of Route 25A, and the end of Laurel Road. (There's an old prerevolutionary church on Main Street at the Setauket Green in *Setauket*, west and north of Port Jefferson.) And *Riverhead* offers a good many places to explore.

Sag Harbor, a National Historic District, is certainly one of the best preserved old villages on Long Island, with hedges and picket fences and curving, crooked, and shaded streets that are lined with charming houses.

Starting at the waterfront, walk along Bay Street and on to the Long Wharf, observe the coastal activity, and inspect the waterfront, shop at any one of the numerous little stores and markets in the area or stroll in the Marine Park or yacht club area. If you wish, look across the harbor from the North Haven Bridge to Shelter Island in the north. Then walk up Main Street as far as you like. The finest example of Greek Revival architecture in New York State, built in 1845, now houses the revitalized Whaling and Historical Museum which attracts more than 35,000 people seasonally. Across the side street is the Hannibal French house, a large Victorian mansion, now painted a pleasant willow color, also the old Custom House, now a National Landmark, the home and office of the first customs collector of New York State. Sag Harbor was named an official Port of Entry in 1789 by President George Washington, and a U.S. Post Office was initiated by Postmaster General Benjamin Franklin.

On side streets—wander off on any of them—you'll see many fine little houses built during prosperous days, late eighteenth to mid-nineteenth century. They have simple lines and the style of that era. These residential streets today, since many of the houses have been restored with care, painted, and nicely planted by their present owners, give you the feeling of the prosperity of the past.

Eventually you should turn left and go over to Madison Street between Main and Union streets, to see the Whalers Church, based on Egyptian style and something of a curiosity but now lacking the spyglass-shaped steeple that once dominated the town, blown down in the hurricane of 1938 and never replaced. All the architectural trim is said to be hand-carved by whalers from the village. And nearby, the old graveyard is interesting. A lovelier looking church is Christ Episcopal down the street. Sag Harbor is a place with a special atmosphere.

First there was a little fishing village started here in 1665 by a

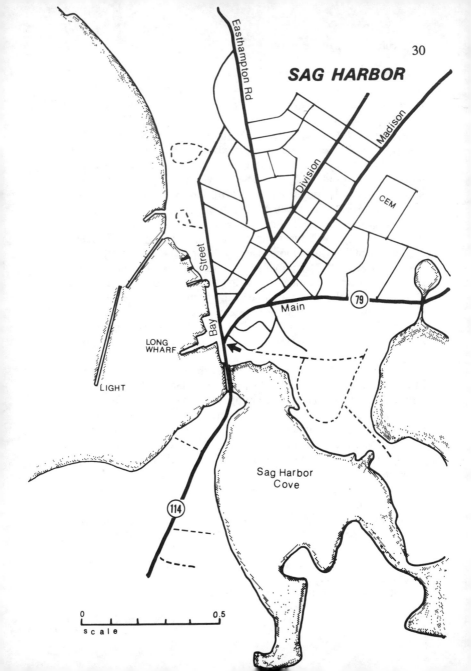

SAG HARBOR

Easthampton Rd

Madison

Division

CEM

Street

79

Main

Bay

LONG
WHARF

LIGHT

114

Sag Harbor
Cove

0   0.5
s c a l e

small band of Narragansetts, traditional rivals of the Montauks and Shinnecocks. Then the white settlers moved in around 1707. Although known for a time as Sterling Bay (after the English Lord Sterling), it eventually took the name Sag Harbor, being the harbor of Sagg, a little settlement near what is now Bridgehampton, a contraction of the native place name Saggabonac: "Where the Ground Nuts (Potatoes) Grow!"

At the end of the eighteenth century, Sag Harbor cleared a greater tonnage of goods than New York Harbor, and it was to become one of the principal whaling ports on the Atlantic seacoast, second only to New Bedford. Between 1790 and 1870 more than 500 voyages were made from here, and the whale oil brought back to light the cities and houses of New England was valued at $25 million. There were once sixty-three vessels registered here. The population reached 3,500 by 1843. Rough seamen walked these very streets you roam today—Montauk and Shinnecock indians, but also Fiji Islanders, Hawaiians, Malays, Ethiopians, and Portuguese. Clearly no princely fortunes were amassed here, as in Nantucket to the Macys and Folgers, because voyages were financed as joint stock company ventures.

After the Civil War the whaling industry had a rapid decline, and Sag Harbor's fortunes dwindled. Today, manufacturing has somewhat taken over, but the annual "tourist trade" provides the economic thrust on the positive side.

Old Bethpage Village is a restoration, a composite made up of simple houses and shops with some architectural merit, regrouped here on a 200-acre site ample enough to provide a proper setting for the buildings and recreate the atmosphere of a mid-nineteenth-century village. And it is a pleasant surprise. We think it makes a delightful walk, a lovely switch in centuries.

You will find a parking lot and a reception center of contemporary design. Here there are an adequate cafeteria, an excellent gift shop, and a small auditorium showing a film on the restoration. Admission is charged, with reductions for senior citizens and children. Allow a couple of hours and spend another if you can make the time.

We walked into the days before the mechanization of the farm. This illusion is skillfully achieved. The dirt path we followed is bordered by a post and rail fence; the field through which it ambled lay fallow, but liberally sprinkled with Queen Anne's lace and butterflies. Birds chirped. There was the faint, not unpleasant, organic smell that emanates from a farmyard.

We were greeted at one of the houses by an eager youth who showed us through. It had been a bayman's dwelling. Uncluttered, simply furnished, it set an informal, friendly air to our visit. Altogether forty-five buildings, all original structures, have been saved from destruction and moved here to form a charming nineteenth-century village.

At the crossroads is a general store, with the proprietor's living quarters under the same roof, an inn serving birch beer in the Tap Room, and a blacksmith's forge. By this time we had noticed that all the guides were dressed in clothes of the period. It is not correct to say that they were wearing costumes—the garb is simple, functional, and doesn't at first catch your eye.

The farm is functioning. There are pigs and cows, chickens and geese. The ladies were baking bread, and a pot of soup hung simmering from the crane over coals smoldering away in the fireplace. It was vegetable soup, and the gardens had provided all the ingredients. The flies buzzed, a Canada goose honked, and the old sow lay sprawled out in the mud.

It is an uncluttered, friendly, helpful little valley, and the attitudes of all the people working here make it so.

OLD BETHPAGE

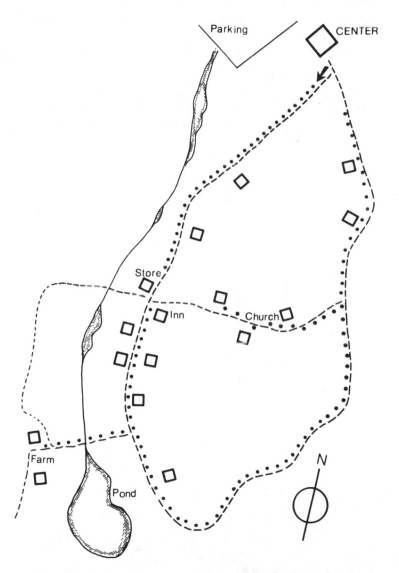

The walk around the loop is 1.5 miles. During the school year we were told there are daily groups—so our suggestion is to come, as we did, on a summer's day. Let the natural breezes provide the stream to float your daydreams on. Lengthen your stride, but slow down your pace, and reflect how downright simple the necessities of life can be. The 1.5-mile walk plus the other exploring footsteps will add up to enough on a hot afternoon.

Remember, though, that the village is open and alive throughout the year, and it is possible to experience a variety of activities having to do with the passing of the seasons. For specific schedules and information, call (516) 420–5280.

"The style of the houses in Sea Cliff," says one local resident with a measure of civic pride, "is what we call 'Carpenter Gothic.'" Perhaps this sets in your mind's eye a village that is a collection of highly individual gingerbread houses on which personal effort has been applied over the years. Actually there's an ample supply of larger, well-maintained Victorian ones as well. You should enjoy a walk in Sea Cliff for surprises! It rolls comfortably over high bluffs overlooking the Hempstead Harbor. Narrow streets running up and down steep slopes, some very small parcels of land, and loving care are the complementary parts that make up a whole picture of Sea Cliff that forms as you trudge around the town on foot.

Start off by parking near Clifton Park and walk along westward on Sea Cliff Avenue. There are some big houses here, and you'll cross through the business district, perhaps quickly sensing that the principal industry is selling antiques these days. Eventually you will reach Memorial Park, site of the old Battershall Inn, which was demolished by the town for back taxes. The property is on the heights, and you will come upon a grand view of the Long Island Sound. Across in Westchester is the town of Rye; on your left is Port Washington.

Walk north on Prospect Avenue, left down Cliffway, and north again on Boulevard. Two sets of steps will bring you back up to Prospect. An alternate longer walk is to go from Memorial Park down Prospect Avenue to the shoreline and follow it south as it curves along under the lovely old plane trees to Scudders Pond. Returning, you can explore the narrow streets along Sea Cliff's "Cliff Side."

The first gathering of people here was really a Methodist summer "Camp Meeting" with tents, picnics, and summer smiles on faces of earnest city folk, singing hymns on the wooded hills above the water, away from the ruffians of the city. That was in 1865. Good steamboat service to New York City was available and convenient from the pier in the harbor. They later bought 240 acres from the Carpenter family, who owned the farmlands, and divided it. This atmosphere was so congenial that people eventually built little houses on their 40 × 60 tent lots to make the camp more permanent and lavished every spare dollar they could to make it attractive.

SEA CLIFF

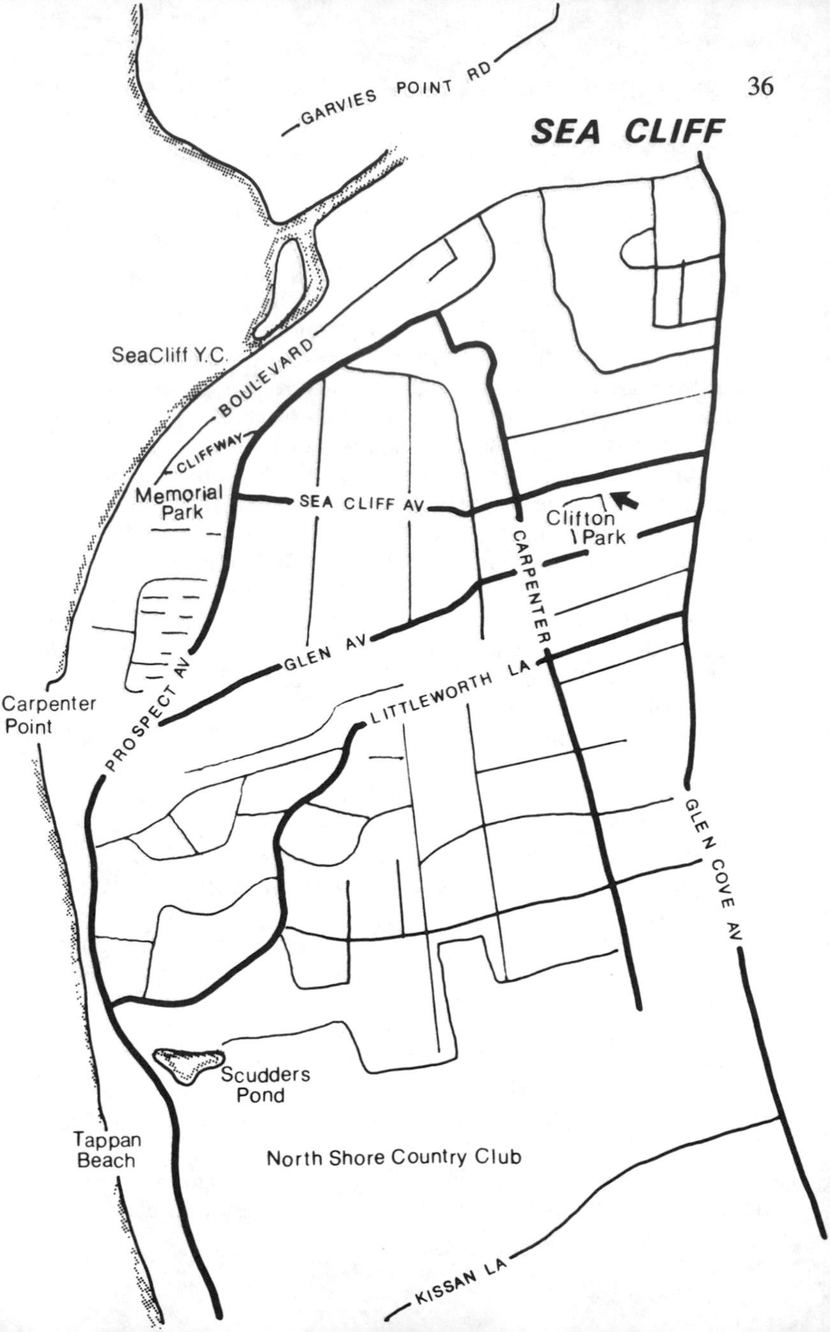

GARVIES POINT RD

SeaCliff Y.C.

BOULEVARD

CLIFFWAY

Memorial Park

SEA CLIFF AV

Clifton Park

CARPENTER

GLEN AV

PROSPECT AV

Carpenter Point

LITTLEWORTH LA

GLEN COVE AV

Scudders Pond

Tappan Beach

North Shore Country Club

KISSAN LA

By 1895, however, word of its charms having spread, it had become a very popular summer resort; large Victorian houses had been built. There was a cable car up the cliff, and a boardwalk had been built along the shorefront. The Long Island Railroad was running trains into the little gingerbread station on a regular schedule, spring, summer, and fall, as well as four boats, daily and Sunday, between Sea Cliff and New York. Nancy Rose, the present village clerk, says for one dollar you can get a little booklet published by the Sea Cliff Civic Association that "covers everything about our community in a nutshell."

The incorporated village is just a mile square, and its present middle-class owners with civic mindedness have preserved and protected its character from encroachments all around. It probably stands today as one of the best preserved little square miles around.

Because Stony Brook is old, handsome, and has a lovely setting and several points of interest, we have included it here as a short walk, although it is not laid out on a grid plan and doesn't have extensive sidewalks. Therefore, the amount of exploring possible here on foot is somewhat limited. We think that you should see it, though, for its unique charm and Long Island bayside country atmosphere.

Our suggestion is that you go directly to the Old Carriage Museum, which is on Route 25A at Main Street, and park your car there. Open Wednesdays through Sundays and most Monday holidays 10:00 A.M.–5:00 P.M. There is an admission charge, and the place is indescribably fascinating. If you haven't thought much about old carriages (and who has?), then you are in for some surprises. This collection, displayed in a perfect setting, is mind-boggling. Carts, cabs, coaches, broughams, phaetons, and wagons assembled here are sure to delight you, no matter how uninterested you may think you are in a collection of old carriages! Man's ingenious capacity to build and skill in handling materials, his inventiveness in problem solving are the basic proficiencies on display, startling you into a consciousness of the continuity of civilization. Besides carriages there are a blacksmith's shop, a schoolhouse and a print shop to walk through, and a complex devoted to nineteenth-century American history.

When you have seen enough, walk north along the sidewalk .5 mile into the village, skirting the pond, which has a great blue heron, families of ducks, water lilies, and beautiful shade trees. It also supplies the power for an old grist mill at its head.

As you come into town, the harbor will be on your left, so walk along to the dock. The bay and spartina meadows here supply as New England a setting to view as any you might imagine. And the waters are lively. It is not difficult to see how the English settlers who came here from Suffolk chose these shores or why it reminded them of their native country. It is easy to understand, too, the overwhelmingly important part played by the sea, the bays, and water routes in the first 200 years of the development of Long Island.

At the head of the village is the small Suffolk Museum, which has a pretty collection of ship models and upstairs, in a glassed case, a bird collection.

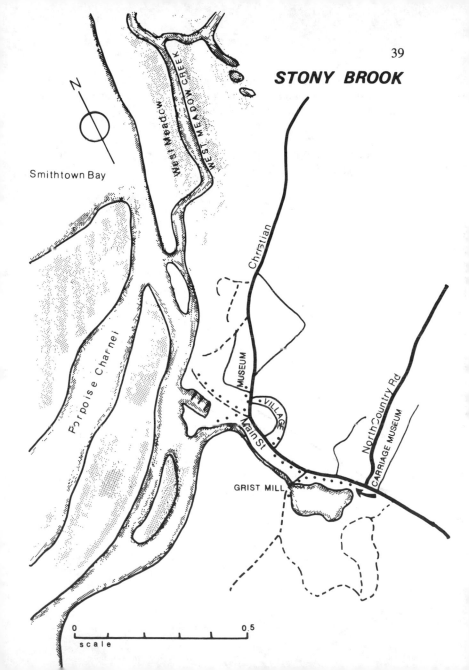

STONY BROOK

Smithtown Bay

West Meadow

WEST MEADOW CREEK

Porpoise Channel

Christian

MUSEUM

VILLAGE

Main St.

North Country Rd.

CARRIAGE MUSEUM

GRIST MILL

N

0   0.5
   scale

The village is clean and tidy and preserves an air. You can walk along window-shopping and head back to your starting point, but surely you will have lost track of time along the way.

Another point of interest, on Nicoll Road south from Stony Brook, is the campus of the University of New York State, an enormous complex of buildings that provides modern university facilities for more than 15,000 students.

Places on earth, like people, seem to develop under current conditions along conforming lines. One airport looks pretty much like any other, anywhere in our world, and cities and houses fall into similar categories. Those exceptions that guard their character from external forces, which have tendencies to change it, and preserve their antiquities develop an aura that is often admirable. Little villages lying somewhere along headwaters tend to preserve this aura, and Orient Village, lying the farthest east of any of the villages on the northern fluke, quite off the beaten track, has perhaps the greatest individuality of any place on Long Island. We hope, in saying this, that anyone will cautiously consider the trust we place in he who reads this. Don't rush right out to look. A swarm of people would be out of place in Orient. Also it is a simple place; you won't be overwhelmed! The houses aren't grand as they are in Southampton or East Hampton. Property plots are rather small, and the antiquities are not on a scale that would attract Sotheby's. It is not quaint, and there are no shops of any kind, other than a small general store and post office, closed Sundays. So you might be disappointed. But for us, Orient has a special character all its own.

If you go, you will leave Greenport on Route 25. The town of East Marion is 2 or 3 miles, and beyond that 3.3 miles, just after you across the narrow causeway with the Long Island Sound on your left and Orient Harbor on your right, is the road that leads down into the village. As you come to this causeway, you should stop at a parking place along the harbor, get out, and look. The map lays out well before you here. The village, from the distance, seems like one you'd see in Vermont. There are snowy white egrets that nest in the salt meadows and a peacefulness laid down on all the scene. We have read that Orient Village until after World War I was a favorite spot for honeymooners. Today it is primarily a quiet resort town. Don't try to drive into town. Park off the road near the war memorial and the white church with the graceful steeple at the head of the lane. Then walk along the sidewalk. Houses, gardens, trees, and reflections will catch your eye. Orient has more than one hundred buildings built more than a century ago. Down the quiet, narrow, meandering Village Lane is the four-museum complex. This sounds formidable but isn't. The Village House Museum, a simple clap-

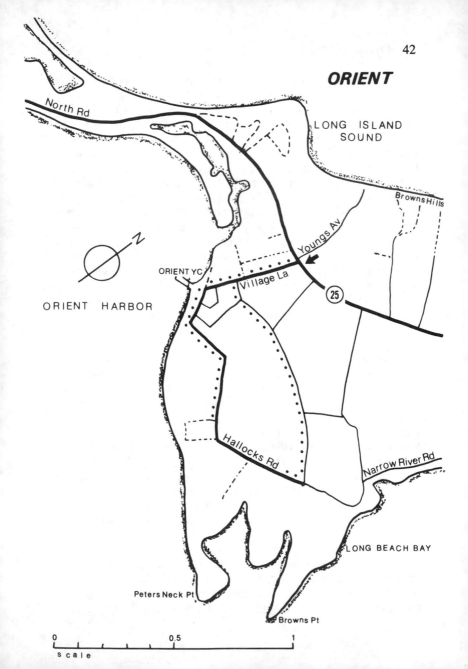

42

ORIENT

board structure with a long widow's walk, is today run by the Oyster Ponds Historical Society. It has early American furnishings and local collections and is worth a visit in summer when open. Next door on a lawn is the Old Schoolhouse; across the street, the Hallock House. Then there is the Red Barn, and so on. Continue down the lane by the yacht club, and you can lengthen the walk as we do by continuing on out into the country fields and swinging back by a loop into the village.

Douglas Manor is a community of cozy-looking houses set on a peninsula that juts into Little Neck Bay at the eastern extremity of Queens County. It lies entirely north of the tracks of the Port Washington Branch of the Long Island Railroad, and we think you would really enjoy this loop walk, about a mile and a half around the peninsula, along a sidewalk by the water's edge much of the way.

As you follow this sidewalk, you'll sense a pride of ownership here in Douglas Manor. Many of the houses have beautiful views across the bay; all have individual architectural interest. It must be a very nice place to live. Be sure to allow ample time to make a ramble of it. Pick a time of day when you'd expect a quiet, relaxed air over life in a suburban area. There is much to catch your eye here—not only the water traffic one would expect by the numbers of boats licensed to ply the Long Island Sound, but also the wildlife evident in so densely populated a county. A recent tabulation from the annual Audubon Christmas Bird Count for this general area, which one might expect to be at a low point, totaled 104 species and 31,541 individual birds counted. Don't expect to see this many yourself—but on foot, if you are alert as you make the circuit, you should see quite a few at any time of year.

If you come by train, get off at the Douglaston Station. By car, leave Northern Boulevard on the Douglaston Expressway and park as soon as you leave the congestion of the railroad station. The loop will take you north on Shore Road with Little Neck Bay on your left, and at the point, around and back down Douglas Road, by the little park and wildlife sanctuary in the marshland east off Douglas Road, to return by Hillside Avenue.

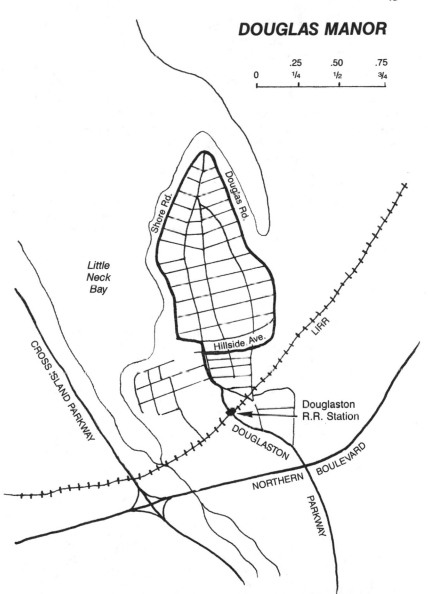

DOUGLAS MANOR

South of the Middle Country Road and west of Calverton is a vast, sparsely populated area, mostly woodlands, with a series of ponds that form the stream that meanders to Riverhead, making the Peconic River the longest on Long Island. It is a long, narrow strip of land on which Horn, Round, Peasys, Woodchoppers, Duck Sandy, Grassy, Twin, and Jones ponds follow one after another north to south. It is an undeveloped series of fire roads north to south. You can wander here without getting lost, and you can go safely any time of year, except during the duck hunting season of mid-November through the first week of January.

It supports considerable wildlife. Deer are plentiful, and bird life abounds. We have seen at least twenty different mushroom species over the years. Although we have rushed home afterward to look in our mushroom guide, we have never done more than photograph them. The great blue heron lives in Woodchoppers Pond. You will see several species of duck, little green heron, a Canada goose family, and, in the spring, warblers, the oriole, the scarlet tanager, partridge, and woodcock. We were thrilled to see the rare red crossbill among the pitch pine and oak. The shores of the pond are marshy, and in the fall the colors are riotous. During rainy periods the trail can be wet in spots.

The half day or more you spend in this area will be peaceful—maybe a fisherman will be here, but we have met only one other hiker in the woods though we have walked here many times.

A good access to these boggy ponds is an unmarked road 2.6 miles north of Long Island Expressway exit 69 on Wading River Road or 1.2 miles south on Wading River Road from Route 25 and just opposite Manor Road. It is a gated dirt road, on each side of which the posted signs read "Cooperative Hunting Area." Another dirt road entry is on Middle Country Road, directly opposite a paved road named Panamoka Trail.

PECONIC RIVER

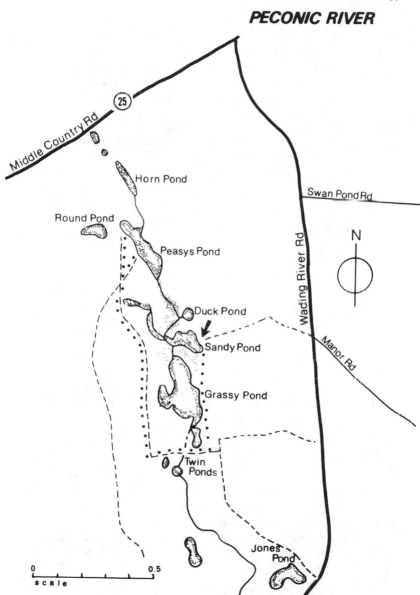

For a woodland walk, quiet, rural, and startling by extensive, Muttontown Nature Preserve is ideal. A marked self-guiding trail runs through an irregular U-shaped fifty-acre parcel of land behind estates. Its trails through the evergreen woods are bridle paths left over from days when all this was horse country. Open to the public as a division of the Nassau County Museum, it is being allowed to go back to nature and intelligently administered. Adjoining the self-guiding trail we describe are an additional 200 acres, fenced and protected, where many of the trails are marked with colored and numbered posts. This portion of the preserve is characterized by glacially formed rolling hills, kettle hole ponds, open meadows, and dry woods.

The entrance to the preserve is at the end of Muttontown Lane, a little road running south off Route 25A, just west of East Norwich and Route 106. And there is a parking lot in front of a simple building, being developed as a nature center. Behind are a little pond that was dug in 1967 to provide better drainage to the wet area here, and deciduous woods of swamp maple, pin oak, and tupelo, the tree closely related to the sourgum of southern swamps that turns scarlet in autumn. Although the pond doesn't support any fish, it does provide the environment needed by a variety of beetles and other insects and attracts turtles, frogs, and salamanders, as well as a variety of birds.

Happily the trails are marked with colored posts, and this is most helpful to guide you along twisty, turny paths where otherwise you might miss seeing much the area offers. Many of the trees are marked, too, for identification. Watch out for poison ivy which grows rank throughout the preserve!

Follow the green markers through the swamp area where you will find arrowwood and spicebush growing, along with ferns, mosses, and liverworts, and you will come out on a large field, once farmland, now let go so that it attracts bobwhite and pheasant, field mice and woodchuck, and turn right here following the green blazes into the evergreen woods. On the hot summer day we walked here the cool of this woods was noticeable. It is a forest of white pine and larch, with a scattering of dogwood and black cherry, and paths are spongy, good walking, so you stride forth with an easy gait.

MUTTONTOWN PRESERVE

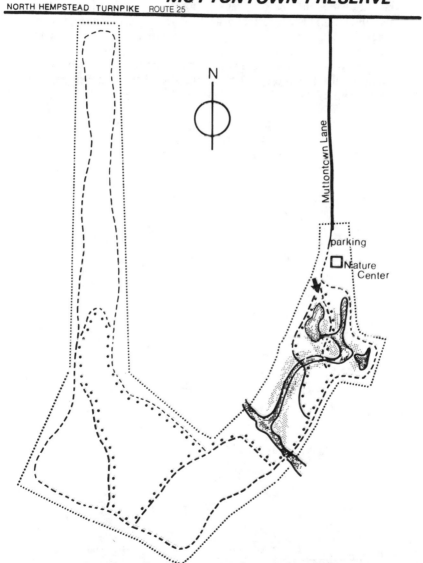

N

Muttontown Lane

parking

Nature Center

Don't be upset to lose your sense of direction. The path actually doubles back, and you find yourself turned around heading north on the green trail, which actually goes nearly back to Route 25A, before returning. Part way along you can cross over on the yellow marker if you prefer a shorter walk.

If everyone who walks here comes as a guest and is concerned and aware of the life preserved here, we shall have a treasured little sanctuary forever wild.

The park grounds of Hither Hills State Park cover more than 1,700 acres, most of it north of the Montauk Highway and little used by the campers who reserve space in the campgrounds on the Atlantic Ocean beach many months in advance. These acres offer considerable variety to the walker, who will find here more miles to cover on foot than he can traverse in one day, so we have laid out an introductory walk plan to allow you a look at the temptations that will make you want to come back again.

There is a large sandy arm reaching well around Napeague Harbor, and though a road will take you partially there, it is another mile on foot out to Golf Point over sandy paths, slow going and too hot for walking in comfort in summer.

A stretch of three or more miles along the great curve of Napeague Bay, pebbly underfoot, is backed by high bluffs overlooking Block Island Sound and with good views of Gardiner's Island.

A lovely freshwater pond in a wooded grove is unspoiled and surrounded by gnarled but stunted oak trees of a venerable age.

And woodlands cover the hills with miles of gradual trails and, if you're as lucky as we have been, the opportunity to spot a few deer.

As you drive eastward toward Montauk, the stretch of highway crosses narrow land between Napeague Harbor and the ocean, and if you watch carefully, you'll see an obscure road that takes off directly north from the highway, crossing the railroad tracks with a proper RR caution marker, and hugs the eastern shore of the harbor. (If you come to the place where the road splits with the Old Montauk Highway forking to the right and to Hither Hills Campground, then you've gone too far. Turn back!) Follow this road and park where the asphalt stops. Walk the path to your right up a gradual slope and to the top of the sand dune ahead. The vegetation is intermingled with much poison ivy. Now keep walking, north and east, down across the sands, up and over to the bay, following tracks in sand. The aspect here is reminiscent of desert and savanna. There are a couple of ponds way out on the point, too low and hidden by grasses, for you to see. The area is said to contain foxes' dens and much other wildlife.

When you come to the bay, walk toward the east and follow along the water's edge till you come to the roadway that cuts down from

HITHER HILLS STATE PARK

Old Montauk Hwy

A T L A N T I C   O C E A N

N

railroad

camping

NAPEAGUE BAY

Fresh Pond

27

Montauk Highway

Napeague Harbor

Goff Point

scale
0   1   2

the bluffs. Then turn south and walk up along the road, keeping to the right and turning on the road to the pond, where you may wish to poke around before coming out again, crossing the railroad tracks and heading back. Instead of following the asphalt road, go ahead on the service road which is marked "for walkers only," walk about 100 yards on this, then turn right and follow the dirt road back to the highway. You'll be about a mile from where you parked your car. The total distance, following this plan, is about 5 miles.

To suggest climbing a hill on Long Island may appear frivolous, but since we have an urge to reach heights and see the view from there, it occurs to us that others may, too. That's why we're suggesting Bald Hill.

The backbone of Long Island is the Ronkonkoma Moraine, starting near the Verrazano-Narrows Bridge and running northeastward through roughly the middle of the island, with the highest point atop Jaynes Hill, 401.5 ft above sea level.

You get there on West Hills Road which starts off Route 110 near the nice old house where Walt Whitman lived in South Huntington. West Hills Park and Picnic Area is on top of Jaynes Hill with a trail leading the few hundred yards on to the highest point. Even on a clear day there is not much of a view. You can see a short stretch of Fire Island through a break in the trees, but that's all.

Another possibility is halfway along the Greenbelt Trail. After skirting the Long Island Expressway at Terry Road, the trail heads up the moraine leading to Colonie Hill, 180-foot elevation, and a good view (but through a locked gate over land owned by Lilco, and you have to obtain the combination through the Greenbelt Conference).

This leaves Bald Hill . . . which is, actually, a pleasant short walk and just may appeal to you. We've been up several times, although the path is obscure, and the first time we tried to find the path it somehow eluded us. Bald Hall is just 3 miles south of Riverhead on the west side of Route 51, the Riverhead–Moriches Road. At the junction of Wildwood Lake, the road jogs and slopes upward for 1.5 miles, and Bald Hill is just here, not appearing to be too much above the highway.

The path in is a jeep road and, as we've said, not easily noticed. You won't have any trouble staying on the path because there are scooter tracks to the top, and you'll know when you're there all right because of the geodetic markers. The view is good in all directions. If it's clear, you should be able to see Westhampton Beach, Brookhaven Laboratory, and farm and woodlands everywhere.

Woodlands are vital—they are absolutely necessary—to Long Island's future, but as in all aspects of nature, the reason for this is not

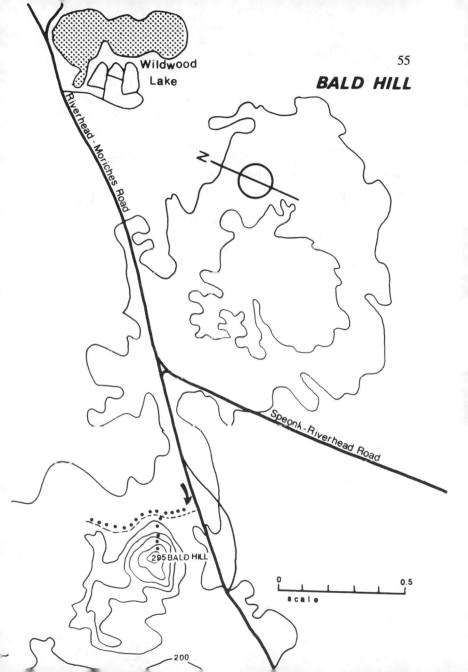

BALD HILL

Wildwood Lake

Riverhead - Moriches Road

Speonk - Riverhead Road

295 BALD HILL

200

0   scale   0.5

obvious because of the most complex fabric which is woven around life. Woods here on Long Island are easier to get at, to cut down, to burn, than in most other places. Roots are easier to bulldoze, too, because all Long Island is just a glacial sandbar. So the speculative opportunity for profit is more so here, close to the dense centers of population, in real estate and for builders. But woodlands build soil and hold it together, acting like a sponge in keeping moisture in the ground. Without water there is no life possible. Three hundred years ago the five rivers and many creeks were abundant in trout and salmon; the water level was perhaps 3 feet higher than today. Most of the creeks dried up as the result of the felling of the upland forest—so you see it's all tied to the water table which has been lowering at alarming rates.

You'll find a road leading off into the woods. Extend your walk and enjoy it while you can.

Sears-Bellows lies to the north of the Sunrise Highway and south of the Flanders Road but fortunately has enough acreage to offer a feeling of remoteness, complete with two lakes, some ponds, and lots of cover for deer and game birds, including the marvelously colored wood duck. Walking here is most pleasant in spring or fall, but people are essentially gregarious, we have observed, and like to be where the crowd is, enjoy the fishing and boating at the big lake, Bellows. Thus, even when we walk here in season, a few easy strides away from the camping area you lose almost everyone.

You will find parking spaces here, as in all Suffolk County parks, limited to Suffolk County residents with permits. Trails are not heavy traffic areas, and hikers are not discouraged, so if you do not have the permit, the rangers will usually treat you courteously if you yourselves are not a nuisance.

The best entry to the park is on a road off the Flanders Road, 5 miles south of the Riverhead Traffic Circle and a distance of less than a mile to the park entrance. There is, however, a park head-quarters on the Montauk Highway about 2 miles west of Hampton Bays, and access is possible from here too, just east of the railroad underpass on the north side of the highway.

Many service roads make good paths through the woodlands and around the lakes, and if it is a quiet day when you come, the walk around Bellows Pond is an easy one. Our favorite walk, however, is from Bellows to Sears Pond, lingering before returning. The paths are especially nice for walking, pine needles underfoot, wide, and unobstructed. Go north first through woods where we always seem to put up a grouse or two, past a pond on the right that is a favorite haunt of the wood duck, then swing to the left and into a clearing that has a significant rise of land on it. We usually climb the rise and sit for a few minutes because there often seems to be a red-tailed hawk here circling, and there is a view of the surrounding country. We rejoin the path on the other side of the hill and walk about a mile northwestward through sparse, burned-over woods. The growth and vegetation increases heavily as you come to Sears Pond. Go down to the water quietly; the ducks are wary in this secluded hideaway. Across the pond you will see two osprey nests, one in disrepair; the other has been occupied regularly each year on about March twenty-

SEARS BELLOWS COUNTY PARK

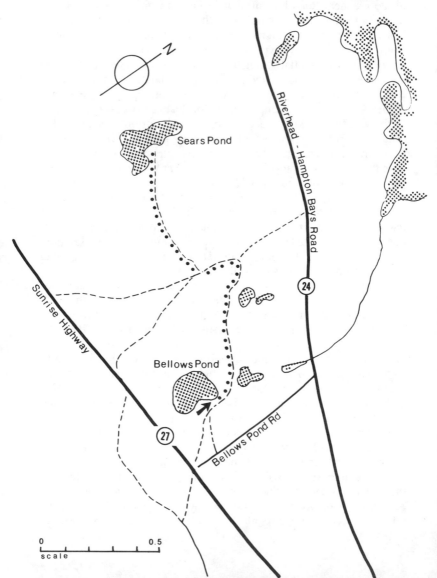

first through summer. If you have the patience to sit in the duck blinds, there are always interesting comings and goings on the water.

Although it is quiet enough to listen to the birdsong and hear the flapping of the duck's wing, the muffled traffic noises from the two highways do carry across the treetops, as do jet sounds of overhead planes on their route to New York and punctuations from monstrous earth-moving equipment or chain saws. This is true, of course, anyplace on Long Island, and Sears-Bellows is as free today of the sounds of our civilization as almost anywhere else. So we can be grateful for the relative calm and tranquility and hope that others, too, will recognize it and strive to perpetuate it. And be thankful for the settings provided for public use by a foresighted County Park Commission.

A rather large area of county-owned land virtually right in River-head is a haven of plant and animal life containing a 211-acre bog, probably the only remaining habitat of this type on Long Island. Although it is unmarked, it is a favorite haunt of naturalists.

The area was originally a cranberry "farm." Now it is held by the county as a preserve and nature-oriented park of limited use. An environmental staff oversees the preserve, but it is open for nature walks on an informal basis. Visitors should obtain a permit through the Department of Recreation and Conservation, Montauk Highway, West Sayville, 11796 (516–567–1700) where, if you choose, an appointment can be made for an interpretive walk.

To find it, drive south on Route 63, which leads from Riverhead Circle toward Wildwood Lake. There are no signs, but there is a chain link gate at the service road on your right, just after Lakeside Drive, which veers off to the left.

Although the park is usually closed, there are a few unmarked trails, and you won't have any trouble walking around the gate. It is a place which makes a fascinating ramble. A bridge has recently been completed over the Little River, and it is now possible to make a loop around Sweezy Pond. The old cranberry fields lie to the east of the pond, and dikes permit you to penetrate some of the jungly growth. We say it is a ramble because to enjoy this spot is to explore, walking here and there along fringes of the wetlands. But we implore you: Walk quietly and cautiously, respecting stillness and wildlife. Deer and heron, swan and geese as well duck, live here, so try especially hard not to disturb. The variety of shrub and ground cover is extraordinary—sweet pepperbush, bayberry, beach plum, wild grape, bearberry, cranberry, bear oak, so many bog plants—and the pond is full of water lilies, slender arrowhead, and reed, a catalog of freshwater swamplands growth. If you like this kind of exploring, you should enjoy a leisurely stroll here.

CRANBERRY BOG

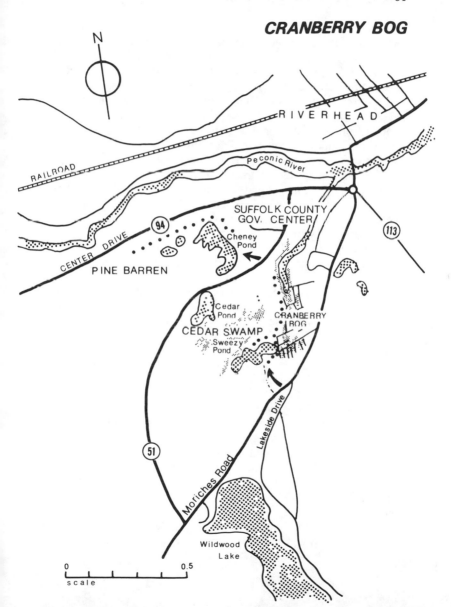

This sixty-two-acre area has about 5 miles of marked nature trails over "the Carpenter Tract," purchased in 1668 from the Matinecock Indians. For thousands of years before this, woodland natives had hunted, gathered, and camped on this and adjoining lands. The concentrated remains of their middens here are one of the reasons Nassau County acquired the land in 1963 and opened the museum, which specializes in Native American archaeology as well as a program to preserve the natural and geologic history of the island. Physically Garvies Point is similar in many ways to the Sands Point facility on the eastern side of Hempstead Harbor.

A parking area adjoins the museum. Exhibits give you a fine introduction to Long Island before its discovery by Europeans. There is a sweeping view of Hempstead Harbor as you stand here at the museum, and the nature trails that start here provide good walking any time of year.

Although in the midst of suburban neighborhoods, the high ridge along the shore may set your mind wandering about the state of the native peoples who stalked along it so many years ago. Those who greeted the settlers on Long Island were generally a congenial and helpful people and at first offered no resistance to the newcomers. Fish and game were plentiful, and they were adept at catching all that was needed. The northern climate here was ameliorated by the sea. Those early settlers recognized the advantages and were joined rather quickly by others who learned about the place. The history of these early days is well documented, and your local library may start you reading about these first encounters between the European settlers and the Native Americans.

During the warmer months, the preserve is full of wildlife; the woods and meadows attract a great variety of birds. Because there's an effort to keep it in a natural state, a wide variety of native plants grow here. You'll find northern red oak, pin oak, sassafras, beech, black cherry, persimmon, tulip tree, locust, sycamore, butternut hickory. It is all in all a very pleasant experience to roam over these unexpected riches.

From Long Island Expressway, Northern State Parkway, Northern Boulevard, or Meadowbrook Parkway, exit on Glen Cove Road,

GARVIES POINT PRESERVE

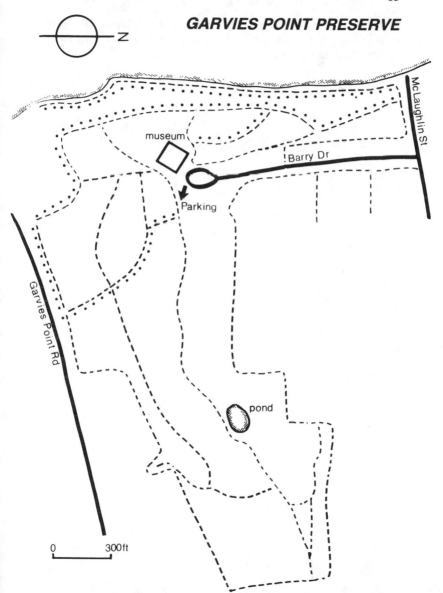

northbound. Continue on Glen Cove By-Pass (Route 107 north, keep left at fork) to last traffic light facing Glen Cove Fire House. Follow signs to the museum.

Just about anybody would acknowledge that John S. Phipps and his wife had the wherewithal to enjoy the art of gracious living. Besides a swimming pool, both indoor and outdoor tennis courts, they had two of their own polo fields! Moreover, they had the recreated eighteenth-century, stately Stuart mansion and gardens to go with it, with appropriate furnishings throughout.

Almost no one can afford to live this way anymore, but it is fun to imagine. And if you enjoy snooping through other people's houses and walking like the Sun King around tended grounds, then Old Westbury Gardens is definitely a place for you. We have included it in these walks on Long Island because we loved it, and friends of ours who live nearby rave about it and come back again and again.

Take the Guinea Woods South exit off the Long Island Expressway. Go east on the service road 1.2 miles, then right on Old Westbury Road .25 mile. There is an admission charge to the gardens and house. You should allow two hours and be sure to do everything, including a walk around the lake.

You enter through wrought iron gates. The grass is tended, and you will not believe the beech and linden trees, which immediately establish an important theme. Old Westbury Gardens is unusual in that both house and garden had the same architect.

The place is continually full of surprises. For example, when you come into the house, there are fresh flowers in all rooms, and the dinner table is set; it is just as though the Phipps family had stepped out but would be back shortly, as though you were an invited weekend guest. The rooms are pleasant: light, airy, homey. And someone with a fine sense of color has decorated it tastefully. It is not ostentatious, but it is a display of considerable wealth—English antiques; paintings by Reynolds, Raeburn, Gainsborough, Constable, and Sargent; gilded mirrors and crystal chandeliers.

Out-of-doors has everything, and everywhere there is delight in the unexpected, theatrical sense to the gardens—looking down on the boxwood garden, coming upon the Italian, discovering the Pinetum. And allees are magnificent!

Now all this is arranged with a self-guided tour and map, so you will have a fine walk of it. Although you quickly get lost—we suspect that it was planned this way. Besides, discreet signs tell you where you are and how to keep going in the right direction.

OLD WESTBURY GARDENS

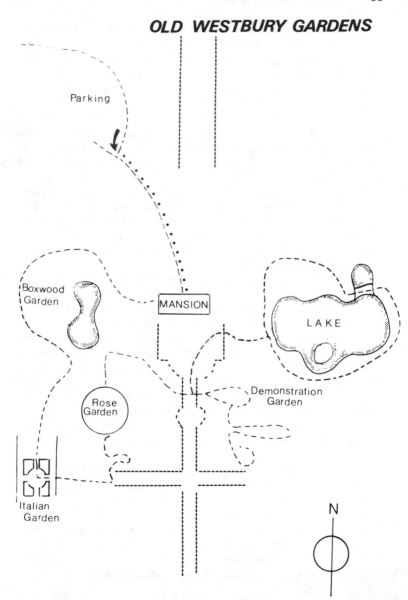

Parking

Boxwood
Garden

MANSION

LAKE

Rose
Garden

Demonstration
Garden

Italian
Garden

N

For anyone with a plot of ground and a yearning to husband it, the demonstration gardens alone are worth the admission. Our suggestion is to bring along a pencil and pad to make notes.

We were happy because rabbits, chipmunks, and a black-capped chickadee seemed to welcome us!

Old Westbury Gardens is open Wednesdays through Sundays 10:00 A.M. to 5:00 P.M. from late April through October including holidays.

Anyone familiar with Central Park knows the genius of Frederick Law Olmsted in grouping trees together. See what he started here on the banks of the Connetquot River on a very rich man's estate in 1887. There are 690 acres with trim lawns and open meadows, a wildflower garden, a marshy refuge, and paths lead everywhere. Along the river's edge, around and through woods, it is difficult to imagine a nicer walk anywhere that has a setting more gracious than the one provided for public use here. The estate is maintained by the Long Island State Park and Recreation Commission, given in trust to the state by Mr. Cutting's daughter, though it is not technically a state park. There is no picnicking, but there is a charge for admission. And it is only open Wednesday through Sunday.

To reach the arboretum, turn east off the end of the Southern State Parkway just before it reaches Heckscher and follow carefully marked signs.

There are five different trails laid out and marked, each with different colors, and were you to take the allotted time on each, the total time suggested would be 3½ hours. We recommend that you plan to spend at least 2½ hours here and make a most pleasant morning or afternoon of it by combining two or more of these walks into one longer one.

There is also a seasonal aspect to consider in planning your walk here. Wildflowers should be out in late March and April, rhododendrons in late May and June. Changing colors are engaging in October. Even on a hot summer's day, however, the welcome release is here; a cooling breeze off the river, shade from the mature trees, and benches conveniently at hand will probably quietly lure you to sit a spell.

The rambly, old informal house is maintained in good repair and partially open. Tea and simple snacks are available cafeteria style, and tables on the large enclosed porch looking out over the river offer an attractive setting for a relaxing break. A fine collection of stuffed birds is on display and should be recommended to visitors.

Heckscher State Park does not offer much in the way of discovery, and so we wouldn't especially recommend it. But because it adjoins

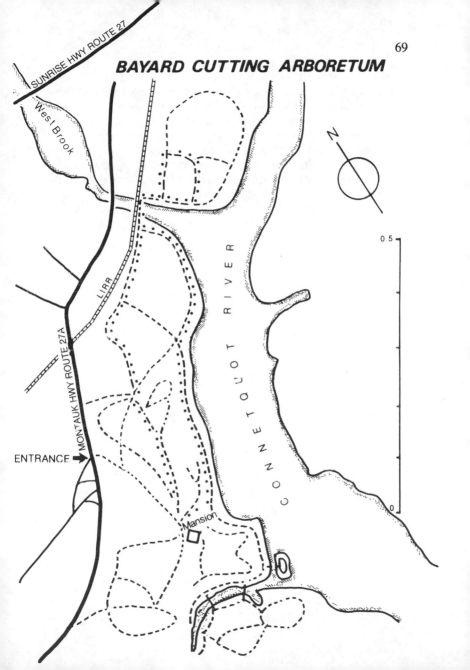

BAYARD CUTTING ARBORETUM

the Cutting Estate, it does call for comment. There are 1,700 acres, and it is easy to get off alone in the woods, away from the vast picnic and playfield areas. It should offer more solitude during times when these fields are not so heavily used as they are in summer. An old dirt service road leads to the northwest corner, down along the west boundary, and out to parking area #5, reserved as a small boat ramp. In early spring you may find it more interesting. Generally, it is a scrub oak woods with marshy places, and you should find wild-flowers then.

East of Old Willets Pass, the large former Weld Estate of 588 acres is open now to the public as Blydenburgh, a Suffolk County Park. You will find parking space here, as in all Suffolk County parks, limited to Suffolk County residents with permits. Trails are not heavy traffic areas, and hikers are not discouraged when the parks are not crowded. Rangers are very nice fellows generally and if you do not have the permit will usually treat you courteously if you yourselves are not a nuisance.

Blydenburg is woodland with swamps and fields, and with Stump Pond, which we understand is second in size on Long Island only to Lake Ronkonkoma. The lake is long and irregularly shaped, somewhat like a boot with a long pointed toe. No swimming is permitted here, but there are rowboats available, and so it is a popular fishing place as well as campground. Several trails, or dirt roads, make for easy walking, and there is some horseback riding.

The best way to get there is from the western edge of Smithtown Branch on Route 25, the Jericho Turnpike. Turn south off the turnpike at the traffic signal on Brooksite Drive and go one block, then west on New Mill Road which leads directly into the park.

Our suggestion for a good walk here is to follow the trail from the house by the parking area down to Stump Pond. The trees near the house have all been planted but are native to the area. Once all this was tended farmland, but it was allowed some time ago to go back to nature. Now plants and surrounding shore are slowly filling in the lake, and everywhere is becoming overgrown. The area covered by the lake is 120 acres, and the fish consist of bass, sunfish, bluegills, as well as a few trout. The plants are common water lily and yellow pond lily, as well as water milfoil. You continue on the path southward across the bridge by the mill and along the western shores of the lake to the stream, which you follow until the trail splits. Take the one to your left, which crosses the stream and goes up the hill, and then follow it back so that you reach the high bluff of the peninsula from which you see a whole panorama of the lake. The walk to this point is little over a mile, and if you wish to extend it, you can continue along the fire road to the southern reaches of the lake, though it is much too marshy on this south end to continue on around. Another plan is to return to the mill, then walk eastward

BYDENBURG COUNTY PARK

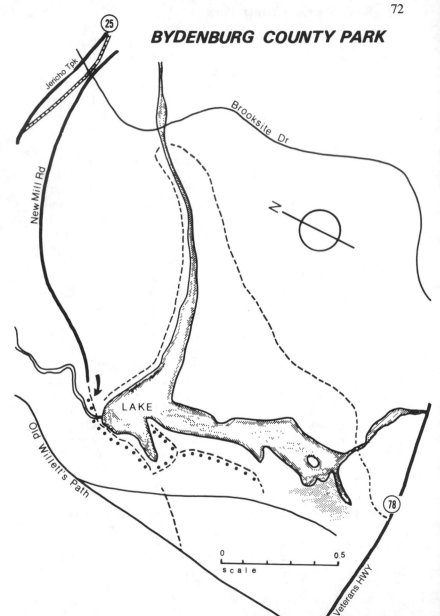

25

Jericho Tpk

New Mill Rd

Brookside Dr

Z

LAKE

Old Willett's Path

78

0   scale   0.5

Veterans HWY

about a mile along the northern shore, crossing the toe at the extreme end, and follow the path westerly as far as you wish. As you will discover, there is considerable variety in the plant and animal life, and we think you'll have a good outing here. In the fall you may see Eastern bluebird, cedar waxwing, and brown creeper in these woods.

Since 1961, 1,500 acres of the original 1,750-acre estate over-looking Long Island Sound, which made up the fabulous English-style domain of Marshall Field III, has been owned by New York State and is today administered by the Long Island State Park and Recreation Commission. And it is a grand place to walk.

A grand place in every way because there are not apt to be crowds, with the many restrictions—no picnicking facilities (so you must pack in your sandwich, bring your own drinking water, carry away your leftovers), no swimming, no pets, no playgrounds, no camping, no driving beyond the parking area at the park booth, a matter of 2 miles to the Long Island Sound.

This gives Caumsett a wonderfully remote aspect once you walk beyond the marvelous old farm buildings and magnificent stable nearby or down along the shore, so plan to spend the better part of a day. It is open 8:00 A.M. to 4:30 P.M. daily. From Memorial Day through Labor Day there is an entrance fee. To get there from Route 25A in Huntington, turn north on West Neck Road to the park, a very pretty stretch of road.

It is hard to imagine that one man owned this vast park and that it was a farm which made its own power and was self-sufficient in most every way. Miles of roads were built for motoring and horse-back riding. There was tennis, indoors and out, pheasant and skeet shooting, polo, trout fishing, a herd of prize cattle, an extensive vegetable garden. None of the buildings is open to the public. They now house the Queens College Center for Environmental Teaching and Research, the BOCES Outdoor and Environmental Education Program, the Caumsett Equestrian Center, et cetera.

You will find here many specimen trees of interest—beech, oak, pine, dogwood, locust. You will find meadows, a salt marsh, and, below the large terrace of the main house, a pond where various waterfowl may be observed, and also the rocky shoreline along the sound.

CAUMSETT STATE PARK

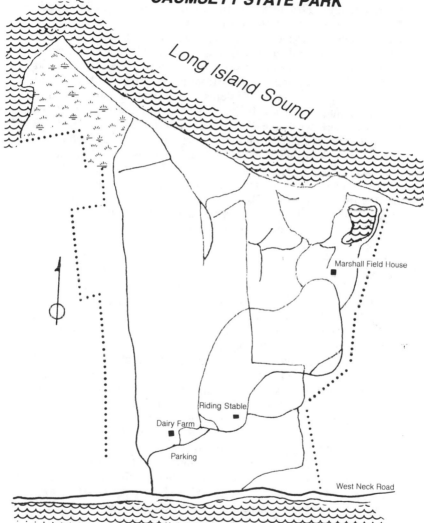

Lloyd Harbor

Comprising 209 acres of prime Long Island real estate, Sands Point Park and Preserve stands on splendid bluffs overlooking Long Island Sound at the mouth of Hempstead Harbor just north of Port Washington. For walkers it has six short blazed trails and a small pond on land that supports a surprisingly wide range of plants and bird life. There is a mile of beachfront to explore as well. It is said that geologists find much of interest along here, in case you have rock-hounding tendencies. In the wooded areas there are native trees that were here when the first settlers arrived and also specimen oriental varieties that were brought in at the turn of the century.

No doubt these acres were groomed and manicured when the Goulds and then the Guggenheims lived here, but they are wild now. There are two old manor houses and a large structure built to resemble a castle, Ireland's Kilkenny Castle in fact, but to serve as a stable. Today this building houses a small museum and also serves as the repository of all manner of interesting items of furniture, carriages, and assorted pieces inherited by the Nassau County Department of Recreation and Parks and stored here. It is worth a ramble through.

The two mansions, one built by the Gould family, were subsequently owned by the Guggenheims. Harry Guggenheim, who was an early flying enthusiast and admirer of the young Charles A. Lindbergh, owned one. Harry's home, "Falaise," was the scene of many gracious social gatherings, for he was an outgoing man with many influential friends. When Lindbergh completed his historic flight across the Atlantic and returned to America, he was hard pressed to find any escape from the mobs who awaited him everywhere he went. Harry Guggenheim gave him sanctuary at "Falaise." The strong friendship that developed between these two, the worldly and sophisticated older man and the inexperienced, shy young flier is a remarkable story, too long to tell here.

Since Sands Point is an easy commute to New York and yet presents the aura of gracious country living together with access to the water and fine water views, the private homes out here tend to be large, protectively landscaped, and very expensive. So it is indeed a privilege to have this fine old estate open to the public. Imagine 209 acres to wander about in where every inch of territory is so valuable.

The preserve is managed by the Nassau County Department of Recreation and Parks and closed on Thursdays and Fridays. Otherwise it is open from 10:00 A.M. to 5:30 P.M., except Sundays when the hours are from noon until 5:30 P.M. There is an admission charge and an additional fee (children under twelve not allowed) to tour "Falaise," the Normandy French country house, which shows its owners' gracious life-style and has been described as a cozy, comfortable place. (It is certainly worth a visit. This is possible by escorted tour only, which lasts about an hour, and it's a good idea to make reservations in advance—516–883–1612.)

Although fenced and entered through a guarded gate, the U.S. Merchant Marine in Kings Point is open to the public daily from 9:00 A.M. to 5:00 P.M., and the seventy-six-acre grounds, formerly the estate of Walter Chrysler, make for a pleasant visit. The young American men and women who have the good fortune to get their education at this beautiful place should count themselves lucky in many ways. They have a stunning 180-degree view of Long Island Sound—the daintily soaring spans of the Throgs Neck and Whitestone bridges and the cubes and rectangles of Manhattan. The campus includes docks with an impressive variety of boats used by officers-in-training to gain the experience necessary to handle any kind of vessel.

There are two places to visit indoors—the handsome chapel and the museum, which features a history of the academy and an exceptionally fine collection of some thirty-five ship models. The museum is open Saturdays and Sundays from 1:00 to 4:30 P.M. (closed during July and on federal holidays).

The academy is located on Steamboat Road, facing Long Island Sound, and a circuit of the campus makes an interesting, easy walk. If they appeal to you, you may watch regimental reviews some Saturday mornings in the spring and fall (telephone 516–482–8200).

As for the training here, it is 100 percent engineering. The graduate achieves a Bachelor of Science degree, a U.S. Coast Guard license as a Third Mate or a Third Assistant Engineer, and a commission as Ensign in the U.S. Naval Reserve. There is no tuition. The age of the students ranges from seventeen to twenty-five. The daily routine begins at 6:10 A.M., with classes 8:00 to 12:00 and 1:30 to 5:00; lights off at 9:45. The school offers independent study and sea training on board merchant vessels. Two graduates who chose other careers are J. Lane Kirkland '42, now president of the AFL/CIO, and Dr. Thomas Nicholson '42, who became director of the American Museum of Natural History.

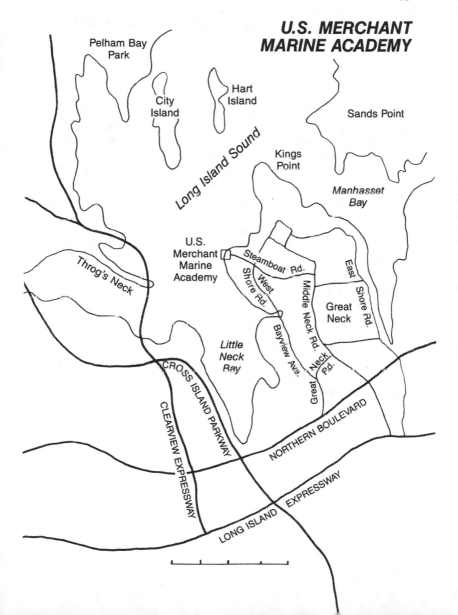

U.S. MERCHANT MARINE ACADEMY

It wouldn't surprise us if William Cullen Bryant had been sitting on the very site of today's Nassau County Museum of Fine Art when he wrote:

To him who, in the love of Nature, holds

Communion with her visible forms, she speaks

A various language.

This was once his farmland, and he loved wandering over it. Today, nature's visible forms still show themselves in nice variety, and a walk here is a quieting experience, even though it lies just off the busy thoroughfare of Northern Boulevard.

The Nassau County Museum of Fine Art occupies an imposing Georgian mansion on a hilltop amidst the 142 acres that long ago were part of Bryant's farm. There is ample parking, and the turn off Northern Boulevard is clearly marked—just east of the overpass at Roslyn, between Port Washington Boulevard and Glen Cove Road. Walkers here should most certainly have a look inside this lively arts forum. There are always interesting exhibits, and frequently musical and other cultural events take place here.

The museum has commissioned over the years large modern sculptures that appear on the landscape and enliven the walks in the fields around the edges of the woods. The best walking for us is along the perimeter road, across the open fields, exploring the informal paths in the woods. There are no marked trails. There is a nice boxwood formal garden near the museum. Were you to bring a sandwich, you might enjoy a picnic in this woodsy setting. It is all so immaculate, it will inspire you to leave no traces of your pleasure.

The sun sets in a splash of pinkish mauve behind the towers of the city. A jumbo jet floats silently into Kennedy on the other side of the bay. And West Pond at Jamaica Bay's Wildlife Refuge is alive, teeming with swooping terns, black skimmers seining their dinners through their amazing red bills, plovers and phalaropes skittering about in the shallows, the great egret and great blue heron standing, majestic in the tall reeds. This is late afternoon in early August. The juxtaposition here of what man hath wrought in the distance with the magnificence of nature in the foreground calls attention strikingly to whether we can keep a balance between these sometimes inimical forces.

You need a permit to visit the refuge, but it is available (free) at the front desk of the visitor's center. The refuge is now a part of Gateway National Recreation Area and hence the National Park system.

If you care to drive (Belt Parkway then turn south on Cross Bay Boulevard), there is a parking lot on the west side of Cross Bay Boulevard 1.4 miles south of the first bridge. Look for one discreet sign. Or you can come by subway. The IND Far Rockaway A or E train takes you there (Broad Channel exit). In case you do, you walk back 1 mile to the entrance. But don't be put off by a series of shack dwellings cheek by jowl on the edges of the bay, sitting upon tenuous foundations. This walk is incidental.

The refuge itself comprises approximately 14.5 square miles, much of it islands and tidal marshes. The accessible spot is the West Pond region, and West Pond is a forty-five-acre freshwater pond. A first trip to the Jamaica Bay Refuge is inspiring, especially undertaken at sunrise or sunset. Those responsible for seeing the possibilities, creating here a forever wild area available to birds on the Atlantic flyway and people via the subway, deserve highest praise and homage. Sit on one of the benches and turn your glasses or scope on these creatures. Many will use Jamaica Bay as a regular stopover during spring or fall migrations. Maybe as you sit here, the short-eared owl will rise from the grasses and swoop about on his nocturnal search for a mouse or two. Even if you don't know one bird from another, the whole setting will impress you.

JAMAICA BAY WILDLIFE REFUGE

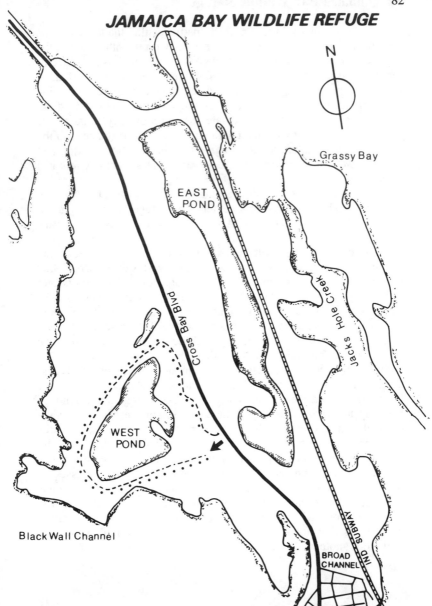

N

Grassy Bay

EAST
POND

Cross Bay Blvd

Jacks Hole Creek

WEST
POND

IND SUBWAY

Black Wall Channel

BROAD
CHANNEL

There are a few suggestions we'd make for enhancing your enjoyment here. Bring along your bird book and binoculars and, if it's a buggy time of year, your favorite insect repellent. Although there's usually a breeze and they may not bother you, in some grassy protected areas, you may wish you had brought it along. Also, eat before you come. There are several picnic tables available outside the visitor center—which is the *only* area for picnicking, and there is no place to dine nearby.

Across on the east side of the road there is another, larger section of the refuge with a one hundred-acre pond and shoreline on the bay as well. Sometimes rare birds stop here, and you may want to look in, if you have strength after your walk around West Pond—almost 2 miles. If so, look in from the northwest.

The mailing address for information is Jamaica Bay Wildlife Refuge, Gateway NRA, Floyd Bennett Field, Brooklyn, NY 11234.

As you fly into Kennedy Airport, you realize that the surrounding area is a vast network of tidal marshes, low lying islands like lily pads in the bay, and barrier beaches conspicuously uninhabited by man, which cause us to speculate on wildlife there. Knowing that the sea rising over a marsh floods this land with chemical riches, that tides moderate temperatures here, and that wildlife in wetlands is abundant, we are intrigued by the thousands of acres behind Jones Beach. So if you speculate about this as we do, then we must recommend to you the John F. Kennedy Memorial Wildlife Sanctuary.

It is a 500-acre stretch, swallowed up by more than 5,000 acres owned by Oyster Bay Town and managed by the New York State Conservation Department, but it provides an opportunity to investigate something of what wetlands life is about. You must obtain a permit to visit the sanctuary by writing to the town of Oyster Bay. Drive through the Tobay Beach parking lot (just east of parking area #9) and into the parking place provided within the sanctuary itself.

There is an old road, just about a mile long, which leads through the middle of the area and provides good footing, although absolutely flat and unspectacular because it is bordered by plants growing to a height just over your head, the usual variety of beach and swamp growth. You can leave the road in several places and walk to blinds or to the observation tower from which you can sweep your glasses over the pond and the treetops, but you cannot get much closer on foot to the water.

It was after Labor Day when we walked here, spent a longer time and walked farther than we intended, and were exhausted. From the tower we had watched a large brown female marsh hawk for some time, quartering low over the marshes, its white rump patch marking distinctly visible, its buoyant, tilting glide a joy to observe. There were clouds of tree swallows swooping about and low cherry trees alive with cedar waxwings. We thought we saw a prothonotary warbler. Glossy ibis flew purposefully overhead. Duck arrived at the pond, skidding in for a landing. Kingbirds and white egrets were common, heron and belted kingfishers scarce.

The black and orange monarch butterfly were assembled in spectacular concentrations. These frail insects are notorious for the long

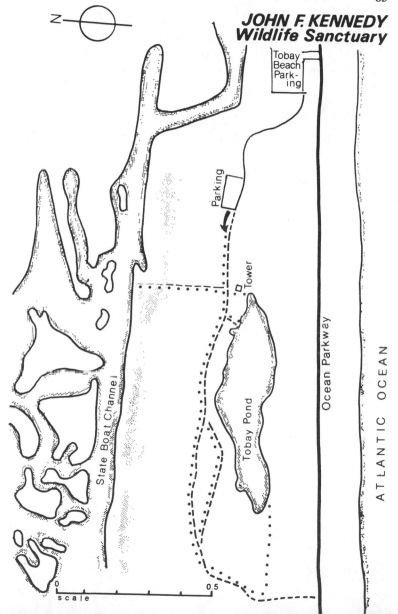

N

JOHN F. KENNEDY
Wildlife Sanctuary

Tobay
Beach
Park-
ing

Parking

Tower

State Boat Channel

Tobay Pond

Ocean Parkway

ATLANTIC OCEAN

0   0.5
scale

treks they make on their annual mass migrations and all morning continuously called attention to their flutterings.

Bayberry bushes were heavy with fruit; catbriar was in tangles. We noticed that birds had eaten the berries from the pokeweed. When we stretched out to rest on the white sandy dunes that overlook the pond from the northwest, we looked up at a sky everywhere interrupted by winged creatures.

Access to the Tackapausha Preserve, just south of the Sunrise Highway in the Village of Seaford, is easy. Turn south on Washington Avenue, go four or five short blocks, and you'll see the museum to the east and, alongside, a parking lot.

This little building is a division of the Nassau County Museum of Natural History and well worth a visit. Inside are informative displays, literature, and usually a nature film to see; and behind there's a small menagerie with Long Island wildlife, allowing you a good close look at a red-tailed hawk for instance.

Surprising is the preserve itself, which maintains eighty acres in the midst of all suburbia. It is divided into three sections—the southern area can be entered just to the north of the parking area, and a trail goes up alongside the Seaford Creek, crosses, and returns down the other; in all a half hour or so walk. Because the stream meanders and branches, there are lots of marshy areas within the main body of the stream, and on the sides are taller trees. It is a good stroll for a spring or autumn day and in no way strenuous. You'll see white oak, red maple, and one of the very few remaining stands of Atlantic white cedar on Long Island. There are shadbush, spicebush, pepperbush, and high blueberry. On the ground are fern and, in spring, flowers—wood anemone and pink lady's slipper.

Because of the variety of plants and insects, there are many different birds at any time of year. A pamphlet listing nearly 200 different species and times of year when you might expect to see them is available at the museum.

There are two other areas besides this north of the Sunrise Highway. The central section comprises fifteen acres and a small pond visited by mallards and other water birds.

The northernmost section is better drained, drier, and has open, grassy areas. It is restricted to limited access to preserve the forty-five-acre area and keep it as wild as possible. Entrance is by permit only. If you're interested, inquire at the museum.

The name Tackapausha, incidentally, is preserved on the original deed for the land in Hempstead. Tackapausha was one of the sachems who agreed to the transfer of land to the early settlers. And that's all we know about him.

TACKAPAUSHA PRESERVE

A quiet place in the midst of superhighways and dense population, Massapequa Preserve offers a pleasant walk of a couple of miles up and back. A crystal clear stream flowed freshly when we walked here; some kids fished at one of the dams, and two boys had a little rubber raft in the stream. The Massapequa Preserve is a wooded strip, drained by a stream dammed in a couple of places, thus making rather weedy ponds, excellent cover for ducks. The walking is chiefly along a dirt road (no cars) that runs along the stream, although there are paths into the woods and around ponds. In August the fragrance of sweet pepperbush permeated the air. We watched a least tern hover and dip over a pond, slamming into the water to capture a tiny minnow, and a family of black ducks float secretively through the reeds. Deep rose petals of the rose-mallow flowers, with their bright yellow centers, made a handsome display along the edge of the stream.

The quiet strip on which to walk is all north of Clark Boulevard, and it is possible to park nearby on Lake Shore Drive, which runs on the east; or Parkside Boulevard, which runs on the west of the preserve. There is an entrance through the fence on Clark Boulevard. It is also a short walk from Massapequa Park Railroad Station.

There are several parks or preserves in Nassau County with similar characteristics, long and narrow in shape and including a stream and a pond or two, not the sort of property that developers look for. They provide drainage and some wetlands and are set aside as green space. That much at least the ecologists and nature enthusiasts have been able to get across. And they really are an asset. It's another matter, however, when it comes to taking care of this precious greenery. Preserves or parks are beautifully kept only where civic pride is a reality. For the most part our senses have not been awakened to the terrible affront the carelessly tossed bit of plastic or, most blatantly, the beer can represents.

As we walked through the sweet smelling lane in the Massapequa Preserve, we wondered why it was so carelessly regarded, why so many beer cans had been left behind, why we have failed to instill awareness in our children. What happened to the Boy or Girl Scouts who scoured this area? Where is the point of pride to keep it beautiful? Do sheer numbers of people living closely together necessarily

MASSAPEQUA PRESERVE

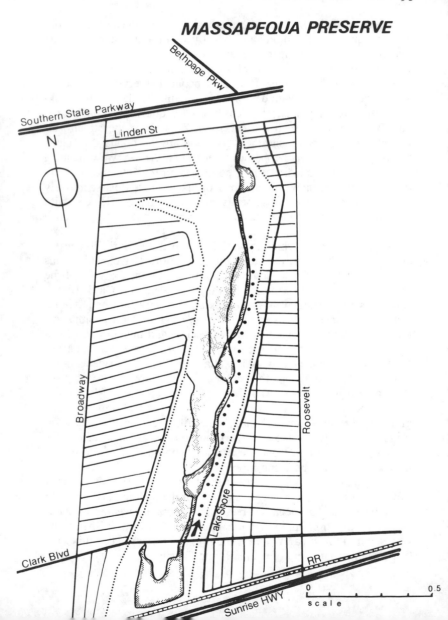

obliterate everyone's sensitivity? Will communities carelessly ignore the fragrant sweet pepperbush and the dainty bright orange jewelweed and all other plants and flowers that can makc a Massapequa Preserve an oasis only if respected? How long can we ignore the careless habit of litter anywhere?

This walk along the stream can be a delightful surprise, however, and we recommend it. If you wish, you may extend it further by following the footpath along the east side of the Bethpage State Parkway, which begins here and runs right to Bethpage State Park (about 1.5 miles).

The New York State Department of Environmental Conservation has had, since 1952, a long-term lease to manage the refuge, a 200-acre parcel that is headwaters and drainage basin of the Quantuck Creek. This provides varied wetlands—swamp, freshwater bog, pot holes, and ponds as well as a tidal estuary. Also there are prostrate pine barrens. Altogether there are 8 miles of trails. The details of the way the place has developed suggest a talented and dedicated professional guidance. The sanctuary lies just north of the railroad tracks above the village of Quogue on Old Country Road which runs north of the Montauk Highway and makes its way around into the Quogue-Riverhead Road.

As you come into the preserve there is a pen complex where a talking crow welcomes you, and there are other examples of local animals. Nearby, in a fenced area, are some deer. And wild turkey roam at will in the open foraging area. There are several tall martin houses. The large pond just at the entrance has a permanent resident fleet of Canada geese and varieties of ducks and waterfowl seasonally.

In spring Canada geese families go about training their young, parading in the grass, one parent ahead and one behind, and the little flock between. Somehow they find the living so good here they stay.

Walking is clear cut. You can take the path that goes around the pond or the one that follows the perimeter of the refuge. We often decide to do both. Wherever you go, you will see typical flora of the Long Island pine barrens, oak and pine interspersed with various berry bushes birds like to feed on. The ground cover is bearberry and blueberry, and there are black cherry, beach plum, and shadbush, as well as nearly seventy varieties of wildflowers. One summer we were delighted to find in a boggy spot a small stand of the exquisite, tiny, white-blossomed bog orchid.

There are a number of places to sit and quietly observe, whichever path you take. Very often, on the ice pond to the north, there'll be a little green heron or some mallards. You can explore this refuge with no fear of getting lost.

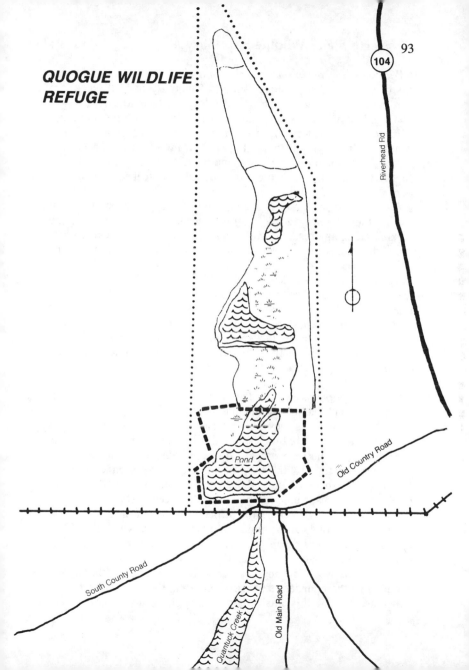

Wildlife preserves are not recreation areas—and we want to stress this because the North Shore Wildlife Sanctuary in Mill Neck is a protected area especially favored, a lovely place to walk, a wet woodland along a marshy estuary that is filled with birds and magnificent trees; visitors are welcome in Shu Swamp and Coffin Woods during daylight hours all year but are asked to observe the posted rules which forbid fires, camping, picnics, dogs, or any conduct not in keeping with the purposes for which these sanctuaries were established.

Although the sanctuary is open dawn to dusk, we recommend that you let them know you are coming, because the only parking (no parking along any roads in Mill Neck) is in a place provided within, and if the gate is locked, you're out of luck! And you can do this by writing ahead. A full-time warden, Mr. Robert Hornosky, is in charge. The address is Mill Neck, NY 11765 (516–671–0283). To reach the parking area, turn north off Route 25A on Wolver Hollow Road, follow it until it runs into Chicken Valley Road, continuing on north to Oyster Bay Road. Turn right to Frost Mill Road, which continues north to a viaduct over which the Long Island railroad tracks cross. The sanctuary is just to the south of the tracks and west of Mill Road. Incidentally, it is just a short walk from the Mill Neck Railroad Station.

We are prompted to write a few words about the tulip tree because the magnificent stand of tulip trees here along estuarial waters is inspiring, towering as they do probably 100 feet high, their trunks tall and straight and branchless for the first 50 or 60 feet. Considered the handsomest eastern forest tree because of its upright trunk and perfect symmetry, the tulip tree is frequently seen as an ornamental and is scattered throughout Long Island. However, the stand here is rare, perhaps unique, in numbers of trees well over 150 years old. Their old bark is rich brown, deeply fissured, and some must have diameters of 4 feet or more. Another name by which this tree is known is canoetree, because the Native Americans made their dugouts from them, and when the English settlers first arrived they found the natives traveling all about Long Island in them. Surrounded by these ancient trees, looking up at those towering trunks, you may see how this was possible—though without tools, it took

NORTH SHORE
Wildlife Sanctuary

N

Mill Neck Bay

The Cleft Rd

Beaver
Lake

Frost Mill Rd

LONG ISLAND RR

Mill Neck
RR Station

Shuswainp Rd

Beaver Brook

0   0.5
scale

great ingenuity and patience, skill with fire, and endless hours to fashion a seagoing craft of one. These trees give you reason to gasp and to consider the wonder of it all.

The North Shore Wildlife Sanctuary, Inc., is, like the Nature Conservancy, a private organization, grateful for your financial help, and contributions are tax deductible.

A spacious parking lot 132 miles from New York City at the end of the Montauk Highway in the Montauk State Park and the weekend specials to Montauk the Long Island Railway runs attest to the popularity of this place. But the attraction that brings the crowds should not dissuade you as a walker. Choose your time and move away from crowds. Montauk is an experience, and you are apt to enjoy it if you are a loner and nature lover. There's a raw bleakness here: hills of shadbush and bayberry, almost endless dunes, and an incessant surf chewing away at the boulders, tumbling stones that cackle in a noisy babble. We've come here at dawn before the sun was up, at least twice, and will come again. If you come at this hour, you won't be alone. Surf fishermen will be here before you. You can walk for miles in either direction. We've been here at midday and at sunset, too, lingering afterward in the twilight. So, although it is wiser to rhapsodize about winter, spring, or fall, our experience is that there's something for you in any season at any hour of day in Montauk.

Where to go? As you leave the parking area, follow the path north of the lighthouse down into the gully to the little pond. Wildflowers, bird of the thicket, and pond life are here. Then cross over the dunes on to the beach and walk south to the point. If you're here at low tide, you can walk as far as you are able. The other direction northwest along the beach fronting Block Island Sound is a less crowded walk, the farther you go, the fewer people and the more abundant the shorebirds. Montauk is a birding area; come equipped with field glasses. There's a handsome new heavy-timbered, glassy refreshment building that serves sandwiches, snacks, and coffee, but if you're interested in food, bring your own.

The Montauk State Park covers 724 acres, so if you walk only those beaches easily accessible from the main parking area, you have not done justice in exploring it. On the way out you'll see dirt roads off to your right. Parking here and walking down one through the woods is pleasant, and searching for the short-eared owl will take you to Oyster Pond. Or another plan is to drive north off the highway on East Lake Drive, continuing on beyond the lake and the airport to your right, to one of the parking places at the very end of the road. From here you can cross the beach and walk eastward toward Shagwong Point, and beyond to the park.

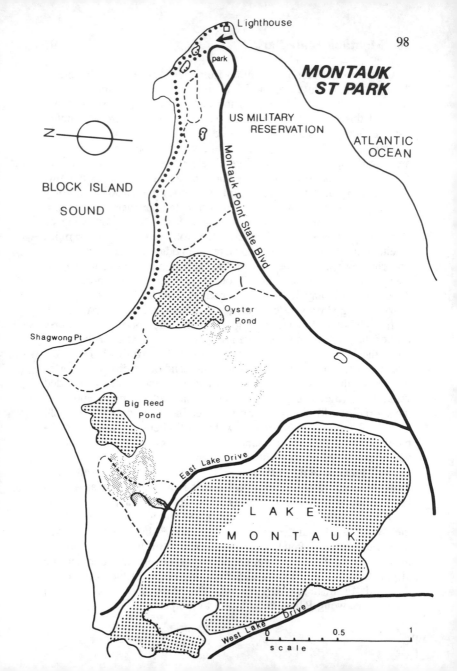

Lighthouse

park

MONTAUK
ST PARK

US MILITARY
RESERVATION

ATLANTIC
OCEAN

N

BLOCK ISLAND

SOUND

Montauk Point State Blvd

Oyster
Pond

Shagwong Pt

Big Reed
Pond

East Lake Drive

LAKE

MONTAUK

West Lake Drive

0   0.5   1
scale

From the bluffs on the point, during the fall migration period, it is not unusual to see the jaegers, petrels, phalaropes, and other species which usually are seen only far out to sea.

In the town of East Hampton, 6.5 miles directly north of Georgica, occupying one of the many peninsulas that jut into Gardiner's Bay and give this area such meandering shapes, is Cedar Point, a choice county park of 600 acres. This is a Suffolk County Park, and you will find parking space here, as in all Suffolk County parks, limited to Suffolk County residents with permits. Trails are not heavy traffic areas, and hikers are not discouraged.

To find the park entrance if you're headed east on the Montauk Highway (Route 27), slow down as you pass the East Hampton Airport. The road signs were not made to be read while traveling 40 mph. Turn north on the first road past the airport, Stephen Hands Road. Continue on it 2 miles, across Route 114; it connects with Old Northwest Road, which bears off to the left. Continue on this to the crossing with Alewife Brook Road. The park is there to the north. Or, driving from East Hampton, follow Three Mile Harbor Road and turn left on Springy Banks Road, which also runs into the Alewife Brook Road.

You enter the Northwest Woods, a high bluff generally 50 feet above the waters of Gardiner's Bay to the north, and drop down alongside Alewife Pond to Cedar Pond, beyond where you'll find a camping and parking area. There are deer in these woods; look sharply in the late afternoon. When you park, you can walk out on the spit which points west. It's a fine walk. And though surely you may temporarily lose your sense of direction, you'll look south onto Northwest Harbor and Barcelona Point, west onto Shelter Island, northwest onto Orient Beach State Park, and northeast onto Gardiner's Island, but eventually the geography of these fingers and watery shores will sort themselves out.

The walk to the point is just over a mile. The inner shore sandy, the outer one pebbly. Or from this entry east along a stretch of wild beach to Lafarges Landing is a distance of 2 miles. Whichever way you choose to go will be delightful, particularly in early spring or fall—summer afternoons can be crowded. Jingle shells, scallop shells, boat shells, or slipper shells and pear-shaped whelks are nature's handiworks you'll find here, along with all the other flotsam that give beachcombing variety.

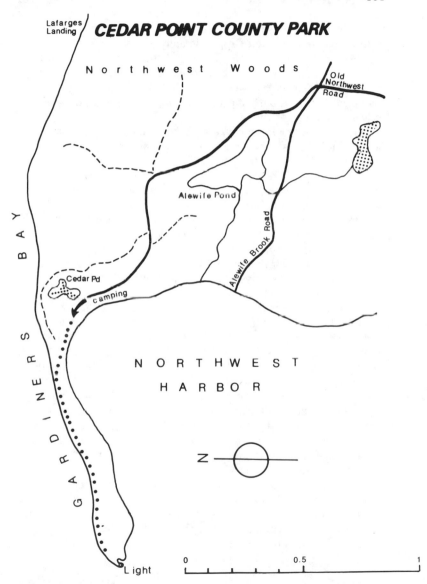

CEDAR POINT COUNTY PARK

Lafarges
Landing

Northwest Woods

Old
Northwest
Road

Alewife Pond

Alewife Brook Road

B A Y

Cedar Pd

camping

G A R D I N E R S

NORTHWEST

HARBOR

N

Light

0   0.5   1

Northwest Creek is protected all around by the county as an undeveloped nature preserve of approximately 337 acres. Though it does not offer miles of trails, we find it an attractive place to park and poke around on foot. The creek oozes out of a swamp, spreads out into prime Long Island wetland, at its mouth forms into a lovely secluded pool of a harbor protected by a sand spit from wind and waves offshore.

You drive on to a large parking area near the harbor where fishermen launch their flat-bottomed boats to venture out into the harbor or sound or bay beyond.

On the left the creek fingers deep into a marsh. When we first came upon this out-of-the-way place, a lady came up to us as we were looking through our field glasses and asked if we had seen her ospreys. It was early April, and she said they were back again, pointing to a tree on the border of the wood at the edge of the marsh and saying that their nest had been knocked off the platform, but that she was hoping they would build again soon. At that time we had never had a close look at one of these magnificent hawks, so we shared her excitement.

On the right is the spit of land that reaches around the harbor, and we find it a beautiful place to walk. Because of what is underfoot, it sets you thinking about primeval beginnings. In stacks of dried sea grasses are carapaces of many horseshoe crabs, the tiniest not much bigger than your thumb, left behind by moulting crab. Actually the horseshoe is not a crab at all but of the same family as the spider, a living fossil whose relatives became extinct 400 million years ago. Then the fiddler crab burrows here in the moist sand among the reeds. Neat little balls of sand piled meticulously beside his burrow look as though he had a machine to turn them out exactly calibrated. At low tide it is clear that the marsh is groaning with abundant nourishment for birds and fish.

There is really no particular path to follow to the bay here; step wherever you can. An old pair of sneakers is the best footgear, because although damp, it isn't necessary to wade. The beach proper is narrow with an array of scallop shells that sea gulls drop. Often the whole operation is so neat that the two parts of the shell

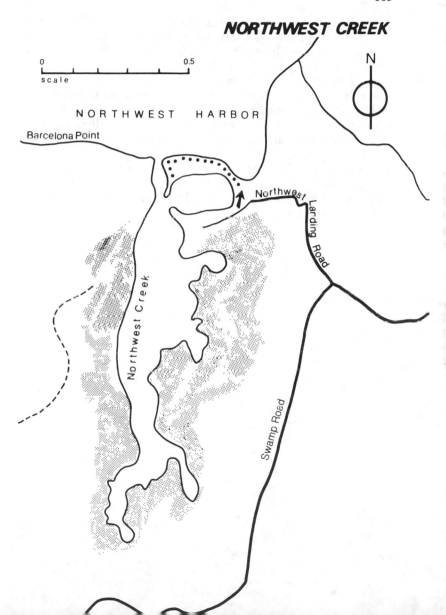

NORTHWEST CREEK

N

0   scale   0.5

NORTHWEST   HARBOR

Barcelona Point

Northwest Landing Road

Northwest Creek

Swamp Road

are still together after the gull has extracted his dinner. At the east end the beach is low with tidal pools, but as you walk westward toward the inlet and Barcelona Point, the dunes get higher, perhaps put there when they dredged the inlet after a storm. You can walk all the way around the edge of the beach and back to the little harbor, making an elongated circle. The preserve supports a great variety of local wildlife, and naturalists have observed, among other birds, marsh hawks, screech owls, warblers, and thrashers. It is relatively an undisturbed treasure trove of the things Rachel Carson talks about so eloquently in her book *The Edge of the Sea.*

To get to Northwest Creek, turn north on Stephen Hands Path at Georgica, then follow Northwest Road to the very end. It twists and turns, goes through miles of pine, and you hope that it will stay this way for a long time.

At the end of Route 24 on the north fork of Long Island, just before you get to the water and the ferry to New London, on your right is the usual rustic state park sign for Orient Beach—but Orient Beach is not a usual state park. Turn and drive along the causeway to the parking lot. If it's spring or early summer, look to your right as you go along the causeway for the osprey nest across the water. A faithful pair returns yearly, and they are magnificent birds, these fish hawks. Sometimes you can watch them fish, diving from on high and catching a fish as much as 10 feet below the surface with their talons.

There is a parking fee in the summer, a crowded time and not one we particularly recommend, because when you walk from the parking lot out on to the beach and turn to your right, you'll find it is a favorite picnicking and swimming spot. However, 100 yards past the life guard you escape the bulk of the crowd. As you move around the curve of the beach, you have the choice of keeping to the edge of the water or following the jeep tracks into the interior of this spit. You may be confused because Orient Point looks to the northeast, but this narrow strip of land that is Orient Beach, 4 miles long, runs to the southwest.

What makes it unusual? It affords beautiful views of Gardiner's Bay and Shelter Island Sound. Wander at will amongst the scrub pine for you are never far from salt water on either side. There are two ponds in the interior that attract water birds, and here among the stunted pines and wetlands there is a herd of deer that comes and goes to the mainland. Although we have seen their tracks many times, we have actually seen the deer only fleetingly in winter. You cannot be quiet enough to surprise these wily, graceful creatures, but how they can conceal themselves in this narrow quarter is a mystery. They blend in and get lost as nature intended.

A good plan is to go out by the beach, pebbly but not bad footing, and back through the interior. If you get as far as the tip, you will come to an old foundation of the Orient light, which guided fishing boats into Greenport.

The place is out of this world. On a February 6th when we walked out to the point, the sky was clear and the Apollo 14 mission

ORIENT BEACH STATE PARK

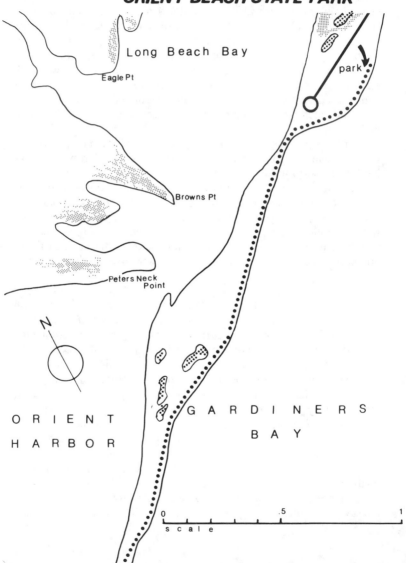

had landed on the moon. The refreshment building was boarded up, and the ground was frozen. The sun was low, the moon stood out clearly in the dark afternoon sky, and the question arose: What is there in the nature of man that compels him to walk a lonely beach, to spy on wild creatures, to search to find the undisturbed places beyond?

The southwest tip of Great Hog Neck is a low lying, beautifully arched beach and salt meadow set aside as Cedar Beach Point County Preserve. It is remote, a good distance east on the north fork, and well off the arteries of main highways. Great Hog Neck is an odd-shaped peninsula between Little Peconic Bay and Shelter Island Sound, with its devotees and many fine summer homes.

Cedar Beach Point is no dramatic sweep of sand. It does have a quality and spirit all its own, however, so that we have found ourselves walking here again and again along the edges of the bay. The large parking lot requires a Southold permit and is crowded in summer, but our walks here have been limited to the other times of year when we never encounter more than a car or two.

The way to get here is not direct. You turn south off Route 24 after leaving Peconic, headed east, on the first road right, South Harbor Road, then left and follow around south again on Bay View Road till it curves at the point. The parking lot is at the place where the beach curves westward to an inlet about a mile beyond, so follow along here by the water's edge and come back on the sandy upper beach. It's a beach of shells, unusual on Long Island which is not noted for the variety of shells. But of those few species that abound there is a tremendous range of shape and color. Millions of baby's cradles or boat shells heaped upon each other in wind rows form the tideline. There are jingle shells like translucent flower petals in their array of yellow and orange to ivory and eggshell colors. One day we collected twelve sizes of the delicate, fluted scallop shell in an equal number of colors. Then, at low tide, the marshy areas are dotted with the channelled and knobbed whelks that the sea gulls bring to feast upon. These are the little monsters whose rasplike tongues can suck a helpless clam from his shell and devour him. On a clear day it seems you can reach out and touch Jessup's Neck, which pokes out from the opposite shore, and Shelter Island blends into the background to become part of the mainland. There is considerable boat traffic, too, a variety of working and pleasure craft to attract your attention. The salt marsh to the back, with the tide of clear waters rushing in and out through the narrow inlet, is fascinating, and you can continue right to sit behind a lovely dune, sheltered and catching

CEDAR BEACH POINT

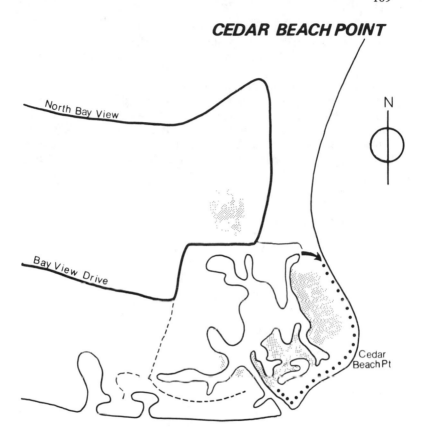

North Bay View

Bay View Drive

N

Cedar Beach Pt

LITTLE PECONIC BAY

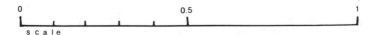

0   0.5   1

scale

the sun all day, eventually retracing your footsteps. But you'll tarry because of the bird activity in the marsh; certainly the greater yellowlegs bobbing in the shallows as is their strange habit will draw your attention.

Because the elevation of land is not ever far above the sea and there is so much cleared farmland at the east end of Long Island, the sky is a real eminence out here. You realize how little you see of it in a city. The sky plays a vital part in setting the mood of each day, influences the aspect of the beach, subtly puts its mark on sand and sea. By special emphasis it seems more brooding, more joyous, more mysterious out here. Sunsets are special—and another reason to lure you to return.

Dividing Little Peconic Bay and Noyack Bay, jutting out from the north shore of the south fork of the island, just above Watermill, is Jessup's Neck. Of the numerous points, necks, and promontories that jut into the waters surrounding Long Island, this offers wide variety of terrains, and walking here is great for many reasons. It is the Elizabeth Alexandra Morton Wildlife Refuge and is managed by the U.S. Government Fish and Wildlife Service as a resting and feeding area for migratory birds. The locked gate is open from sunrise till sunset.

A devoted naturalist tends the place. The office is in the little building to the right beyond the parking area, and you'll probably be able to ask any questions you have. Walking, you can spend an hour or a day, come back again and again, never tire of the combination of beach, pond, woods, and wetlands here.

The refuge is 8 miles northeast off the Montauk Highway, exit 8, in Southampton, and the way is well marked. Follow along toward North Sea, and you will drive into the grounds through a gate on the northern side of Noyack Road; park here near an old barn a few hundred yards beyond. Register in the little hut which has a map and pictures.

The path down to the bay is about a half mile and planted with many kinds of berry bushes—delectables for the land birds who frequent this quiet sanctuary. There is honeysuckle, myrtle, and rural charm. Be quiet and alert. We have come down this path on an early evening and surprised a graceful doe feasting on these same bushes. The path emerges upon a long narrow strip of beach on the bay with a small inlet from the bay on the right. This area supports some 500 black duck who winter here.

Birds are in the inlet, and now and then a clammer leans out of his boat to scoop the bottom with his clamming rake. There will be the occasional boating party pulled up on the beach to swim. In fall or winter you'll see scallop boats in the bay dragging, though these juicy morsels are dwindling alarmingly, and nowhere else in the world does such a tiny, sweet, tender scallop exist.

You walk directly north about a mile and a half and come to a sharp rise and spread of land on a wooded promontory. We like to

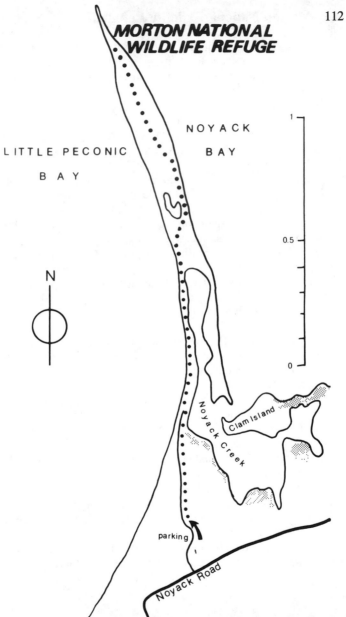

MORTON NATIONAL
WILDLIFE REFUGE

NOYACK

BAY

LITTLE PECONIC

BAY

1

0.5

0

N

Noyack Creek

Clam Island

parking

Noyack Road

walk in the woods on the path then return by the beach. At present the path through the second bluff is closed due to osprey nesting on the east side and probably will remain so for some time. At the beginning of the wooded path there was once a farmhouse. In the spring a carpet of daffodils appears out of the myrtle, splendid in color in this secluded habitat.

In the spring woods, during the warbler migration you see some fifteen different varieties flitting among the big oaks before the leaves come on. And down on the beach near the pond to the west of the neck, look out to the weir where the osprey often sits on a pole where the pickings are concentrated for him.

The Morton Refuge can be a cool and refreshing place walking along the neck in summer, and in winter, when the bay freezes solid, if the winds across the ice are too chilling, there are many protected acres of woodland to the east before you reach the bay, and calm shelter for a walk under cover. One early spring we discovered a strangely eerie sight of dry white bones in a bed of greenest myrtle, the carcass of a deer dead of starvation or exhaustion. Later the refuge manager told us he had taken the skeleton to a school for preservation.

Incidentally, this is one of 410 refuges managed by the Fish and Wildlife Service throughout the United States—many of them provide similar opportunities for walking and observing wildlife.

A blazed trail winds across the full width of Long Island and has since 1978, going northward 34 miles from Great South Bay to Long Island Sound. This was made possible through the inspiration and initiative of the Long Island Greenbelt Trail Conference, combined with cooperative effort of the towns of Islip and Smithtown, Suffolk County and New York State, and the financial support of a dozen public-spirited, ecology-minded corporations with a stake in Long Island's future. It is a noteworthy accomplishment.

Anyone may walk the trail, which has locked gates at several places, but you must have a permit to get the combinations (516–581–1005, Connetquot State Park). They print a map guide with nine maps that show clearly the route the trail follows, and this is obtainable through the Long Island Greenbelt Trail Conference, Inc., 23 Deer Path Road, Central Islip, NY 11722 (516–234–3112, Nancy Manfredonia).

Whenever possible, we walk trails and loop back, retracing to our car, because any shuttle system is difficult for us to arrange. We recommend to you the end section of this Greenbelt Trail, which traces the edges of the Nissequogue River's mouth just east of King's Park. It is a walk of 4–5 miles—or 6 if you choose. You can park either at the Obediah Smith House (built about 1700) or alongside Harriman Pond Park; both on St. Johnland Road just north of its junction with Landing Road. The vertical white blazes about 2 × 4 inches painted on trees, rocks, and fenceposts are easy to pick up here as the trail winds along the Riviera Road following a curve in the Nissequogue River. Then it turns into St. Johnland Road. Just below the Obediah Smith House, the trail leaves the road and cuts north across the marsh. Go in here at the double blaze. You should have no trouble following the blazes, which are prominent. A single blaze means you're on the right track; a double means a sudden bend.

The path crosses through tall reeds, follows along the river, and edges the eastern boundaries of King's Park State Hospital to come out on the river sands and pass under a dock to the Old Dock Road Park. Then it climbs up to the 150-foot bluffs where there are spectacular views. To the east is Short Beach, which belongs to the

NISSEQUOGUE ESTUARY

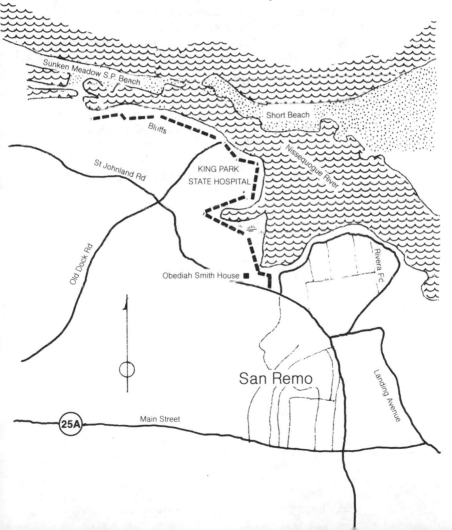

Smithtown Bay

Sunken Meadow S.P. Beach

Short Beach

Bluffs

Nissequogue River

St Johnland Rd

KING PARK
STATE HOSPITAL

Old Dock Rd

Rivera Fd.

Obediah Smith House ■

San Remo

Landing Avenue

25A

Main Street

village of Nissequogue, and Crane Neck Point across Smithtown Bay. Across the sound is Connecticut, of course, and the city with the tall buildings is Bridgeport. There are always boats of many sizes which move in a businesslike way across the sound's waters and, near shore, swans, which have a close affinity to Long Island. This section of the trail provides picture postcard views all along the bluffs, and when the waterfowl migrate, it can be spectacular. The bluffs are popular, so for the quiet moods that the trail does have, it is best to walk here early in the morning—or late on a summer's day to watch the sunset.

The Greenbelt Trail starts off at Heckscher State Park, crosses the Bayard Cutting Arboretum, Connetquot River State Park Preserve, Blydenburgh County Park, Nissequogue River State Park Preserve, and ends at Sunken Meadow State Park, each of which we write about in this book. The trail follows its own purposeful way and is for hikers who intend covering some distance. If you, like us, are interested in a ramble, you'll do better to poke through these areas more slowly on your own.

The Horton Point Lighthouse sits serenely, looking something like a canvas by Edward Hopper, high over the waters of Long Island Sound facing Connecticut. It is the chief ornament of a tree-shaded town of Southold park, which is a beautiful place to picnic. It should be noted that on a visit to Southold as a young surveyor, George Washington recommended that a navigational beacon be set up on this spot. Today it houses a marine museum.

An extraordinarily long set of wooden steps takes you down to the boulder-strewn beach. In all kinds of weather it is picturesque because of fisher-folk. They take blackfish from around those rocks. They dig their poles into the sand, light their pipes, and keep an eye on the floats, ready to jump and reel in when they bob. We always check to see if they have a few swimming about in their pails.

Walking on Horton's beach can be rough because of the pebbles, but good for massaging the insteps. Snorkeling is popular here. It's one of the few places on Long Island where we see people in wet suits with SCUBA tanks and flippers. The huge rocks are relics of the ice age.

There is a long beach stretch here to the west that seems uninhabited, very wide with lots of driftwood. And the flotsam that heaves itself up on a beach is fascinating.

Standing on these north shore bluffs makes Long Island's formation in the geological past become fundamentally clear. You can imagine the great pushing blade of the glaciers, for geologists say Long Island is wholly the result of the glaciers, shoving a wide, wide swath of sand, soil, rock, tops of mountains southward like a massive bulldozer and piling it here. Then the ice melted and the waters ran off, washing the soils southward into a plain. The colossal scale of the whole thing can be appreciated when you realize that the ocean was raised to its present level, more than 300 feet higher than it had been, by the melted ice to form the Long Island Sound. And what capriciousness there was in shoving and raising the level of the waters can be seen in the structure of peninsulas and spits and tiny islands that make up the shape of the map today.

And the force that could bring these huge boulders can be better appreciated when you walk along the beach here comparing your

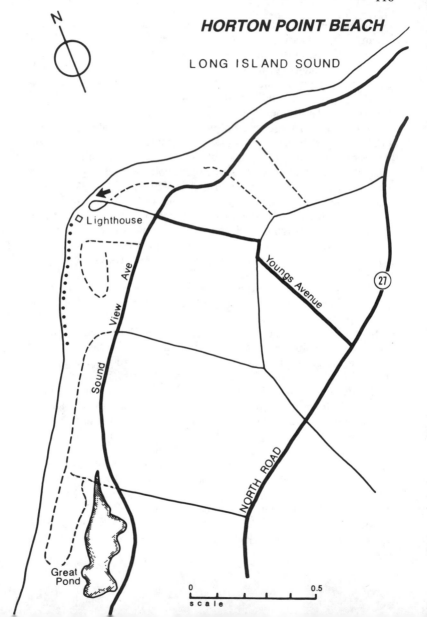

HORTON POINT BEACH

LONG ISLAND SOUND

Lighthouse

Youngs Avenue

27

Sound View Ave

NORTH ROAD

Great Pond

0   0.5
scale

size to their size. Surely the experience is a universal one. One that will linger with you.

A word on getting here. Take the four-lane Route 27 east from Mattituck to the very end and continue on for another half mile on the road toward Greenport. Then go north on Youngs Avenue, which bisects the highway, to the end of the road.

Wildwood State Park is well out on the island, 73 miles east of New York City. It is roughly rectangular and has a frontage a little more than 3.5 miles on the Long Island Sound. Situated on high ground with high bluffs, it covers a little more than 500 acres. There is good walking along pebbly north shore beach here. Also, within the park, there are about 5 miles of trails through woodland areas all amply cleared and easy walking straightaway, fairly level, nothing strenuous. It is a place that is open, protected, quiet, wooded. And you can walk at a good clip.

Many of the north shore beaches are private, not allowing easy access without trespassing, but here is a large parking lot with a broad macadam walkway leading down a gradual slope less than a half mile to the beach. The sand doesn't shift along these north shore beaches rapidly as it does along the Atlantic. The water freezes up much more quickly and warms up earlier in the spring. The ground is gravelly, and there are quite a few boulders, debris of the glacial period. Protected as the beach is by these high bluffs, it is a marked contrast to the ocean shore and offers good variety to a beach walker. There's less severe buffeting in windy weather, too. Those close relatives of the crab, barnacles, have attached themselves to all boulders. Seaweed in many forms is exposed. Periwinkles and whelks abound. The narrow strip of this tidal zone teems with life, hidden between rocks and usually ignored by all except the most curious persons. Wildwood State Park, however, does have a considerable population because of a large tent camping area and trailer camp, so it is a popular weekend retreat and no place to walk the beach during summer months if you seek a lonely stretch. Plan to walk in Wildwood out of season, when it will be rewarding.

To get to Wildwood, take Route 54, Hulse Landing Road, north from Route 25A. It is just east of Wading River.

Quite naturally the inland trails are places less frequented, although they are more protected and easier walking. If it weren't for the trees along the north shore, erosion would have taken most of Long Island into the sound. So walk here to discover the woodland, the home of numerous insects, birds, and mammals, and bring along a curiosity to get to know still another tree, shrub, or creature with whom we share the earth.

WILDWOOD STATE PARK

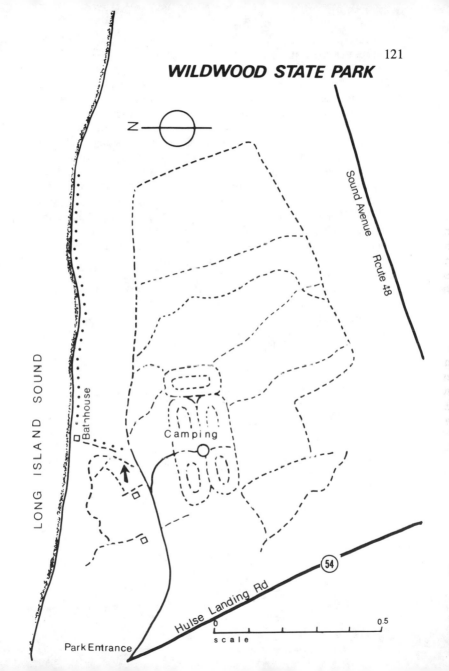

N

Sound Avenue

Route 48

LONG ISLAND SOUND

Bathhouse

Camping

Hulse Landing Rd

54

0   0.5
s c a l e

Park Entrance

The town of Riverhead maintains a beach at the end of Roanoke Avenue on Long Island Sound. Off season, there is usually no problem parking, though during summer months a permit is required (obtainable at the town recreation department). The bluffs on the sound are extremely high, the beach at the tide line quite pebbly and, just west a half mile, strewn with two ship hulks, wrecks of some time past. It's a steep walk down to the beach from the parking spot. Turn left and walk a couple of hundred yards, and you will be alone.

For miles along here the border of high wooded bluffs obscures any houses, and there is a feeling of immense loneliness. There are especially wide areas and big tangles of the purple beach pea, sea rocket, and bishop's weed. Some reeds at the base of the bluffs are so tall you can be completely concealed by them. It is nice exploring territory. Tangles of growth conceal old driftwood, and there are wild beach flowers. Fishing offshore here must be pretty good; there are frequently clusters of small boats bobbing not far out and an occasional surfcaster.

We have walked this beach many times, but never during swimming season. Its setting—the beach is tucked down under a high ridge—

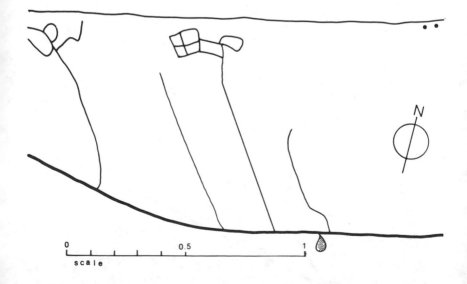

appeals to us. In a winter rain the Connecticut shoreline is completely obscured. With snow on the frozen ground you cover distances faster. In early spring we find trailing arbutus on paths up the bluffs, with winter green and partridge berry. The trailing arbutus is particularly satisfying to come upon in blossom, such a delicate fragrance and the tiny, palest lavender petals. On fresh, bright sunny weekends, the promise of a good breeze brings many sails out on the sound, and the clarity lets you see details on the opposite shores. Falling autumn leaves pile up in the gullies, cover paths, and rustle when you pass along. Because we never have any particular objective in mind, we always look at a watch as we start off headed west, and when we remember to look again, we are always surprised by the lateness of the hour. We usually take along field glasses and a camera.

How to get there? Follow Roanoke Avenue north until it ends at Sound Avenue. Then turn left, west, and go a short distance up the first road, Park Road. Turn right, north, and follow up and down a hill or two. The road stops in a parking area that overlooks Reeves Beach.

REEVES BEACH

Sunken Meadow State Park is a grand beach for walkers, but most particularly when it's not swimming weather, for then it's a grand beach for swimmers. Take a nice, crisp fall weekend to go or a soft spring day or even a misty summer's day for there are miles to explore, with an interesting inlet to the east and a bridle path to the south.

This beautiful beach—one of the nicest sand beaches on the North Shore—and salt marsh were opened to the public back in the 1920s when the legendary Robert Moses acquired an abandoned estate, seeing its possibilities for a public recreation area on the sound directly north of a state park on the ocean which bears his name. There are five large parking lots, copious picnic areas and playgrounds, plus a couple of refreshment stands. Sunken Meadow is a highly organized place for beach activities, but all this quiets down in the off season.

If you walk eastward toward the inlet, you will be on a peninsula. From here you see the bluffs along which the Greenbelt Trail winds and then comes down to end at parking lot #4. You also see fishermen in almost any weather, clammers, and quiet, more protected waters to the lee.

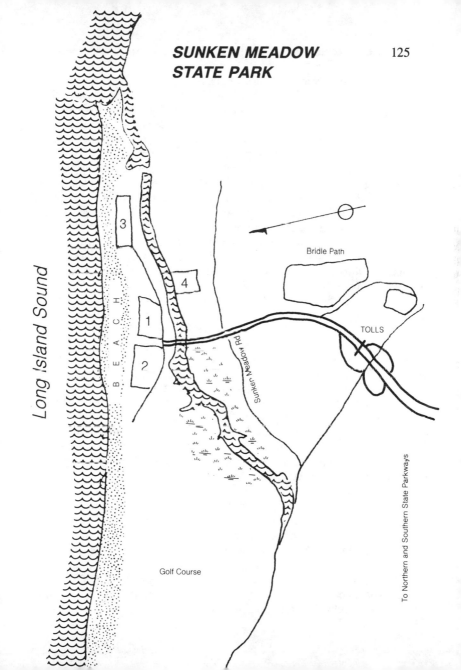

SUNKEN MEADOW STATE PARK

Long Island Sound

B E A C H

3

4

1

2

Bridle Path

Sunken Meadow Rd

TOLLS

Golf Course

To Northern and Southern State Parkways

Connetquot River State Park Preserve is an ideal place to walk. It has a very special place in the Long Island State Park system; the designated term "preserve" means that there are no ball fields or playgrounds or picnic areas. The idea is to keep an area like this much as it has always been and to limit its use to "passive recreation," such as walking, horseback riding, fishing.

It is necessary to have a permit to enter, which is obtainable by applying in advance in writing: Long Island State Park and Recreation Commission, Administration Headquarters, Babylon, NY 11702—easy to do and well worth it. The effort is too great for many who would probably not appreciate or respect the charm of it all.

A word about getting to its obscure entrance off the Sunrise Highway, Route 27, which is a double two-lane highway, each headed in opposite directions. You must be on the westbound lane, so if you are headed east, it is necessary to get off and transfer lanes, which can be accomplished beyond Connetquot Avenue at the Oakdale exit.

An explanation of how an oasis this size, nearly 3,500 acres, is possible is in the deed, which was held by a syndicate of wealthy sportsmen as a private trout stream and hunting preserve for well over one hundred years. Before that, it was held as a patent dating back to prerevolutionary times. When you leave your car at the parking lot and stroll out by the buildings near the entrance booth, you will be seeing what was the clubhouse and what has been available to public access only since 1978. In days gone by, others who have walked these trails that you just might have heard of include Daniel Webster, Ulysses S. Grant, General Sherman, Lorenzo Delmonico, and Charles L. Tiffany, to name a few—membership was limited to one hundred names at any time.

We headed out on the red blazed trail—there are miles and miles of trails—catching glimpses of the Connetquot River as we went along. It was late November, and all the migrating birds had passed through, but we saw hooded merganser, mallard, swan, and a female wood duck. We saw three deer, surprised two rabbits, a squirrel, and a fox.

"It was a red fox. We have them here," Gil Bergen, the park superintendent who has managed the place for many years, told us. "You are lucky to see one in the daytime."

CONNETQUOT RIVER STATE PARK PRESERVE

IIIIIII Greenbelt Trail
— — — Blue Trail
▬ ▬ ▬ Red Trail

Bunches Bridge

Hatchery

Main Pond

Sunrise HWY

Parking

Slade Pond

27

Montauk HWY

27A

Oakdale

Connetquot River

Similar to Connetquot, the Nissequogue tract of land, 543 acres, was held by a wealthy Brooklyn group, organized in 1872 and a short time later named the Wyandanch Sportsman's Club. It was used for fly-fishing as well as bird shooting. Today it is open for "passive recreation" as an environmental preserve. And you must have a permit, which can be obtained by phone (516–265–1054) or by writing.

This tract is bisected by the Jericho Turnpike (Route 25) which runs in a curve southwesterly here, and the entrance, which is obscure, is off the northern side of the highway 3 miles east of the Sagtikos State Parkway (2 miles west of Smithtown). Drive slowly and keep a sharp lookout through this heavily wooded section of the road; otherwise you could easily miss it. There is a parking fee.

Nissequogue River State Park Preserve is the location of the Aron Vail House, which was an inn on the old stagecoach route and a point of interest in early Smithtown history. And on the rise of ground the large administration building houses interesting wildlife displays that will set the tone for your ramble through the territory. Drained by streams and ponds, it is made up of swamp and upland and provides a fine habitat for many geese and ducks, a wide variety of birds, rabbits, raccoons, and native wildlife. We found the undulating trail soft and pleasant footing, remarkably quiet in one of the busiest sections of Suffolk County.

On our walk here we followed the trail blazed for cross-country skiing and stayed entirely on the northwest side of the preserve. These rolling slopes and hillsides are the northern side of the Ronkonkoma Moraine, and the drainage flows southerly into the Nissequogue River, which is within the southeasterly section of the preserve and flows into the Long Island Sound.

We suggest you check in at the administration office for advice on where to walk. It is possible to explore other areas. The objective of the officials is to accommodate reasonable public use and to maintain the status quo of the natural conditions here. Someone at the office will probably suggest something of particular interest to you.

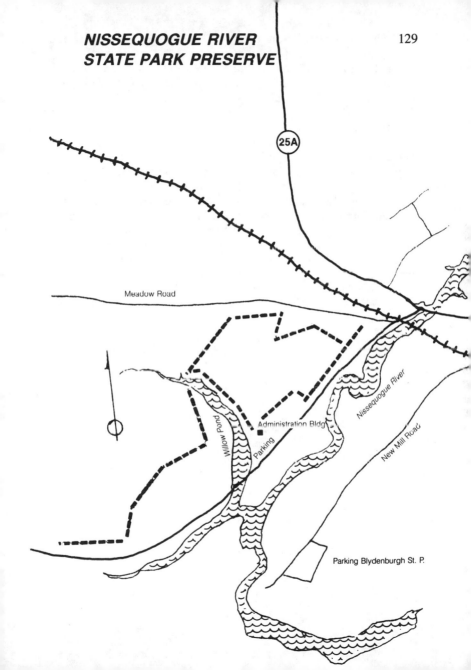

NISSEQUOGUE RIVER STATE PARK PRESERVE

25A

Meadow Road

Willow Pond

Administration Bldg

Parking

Nissequogue River

New Mill Road

Parking Blydenburgh St. P.

51 Uplands Farm Sanctuary 130

The Long Island Chapter of the Nature Conservancy has its head-quarters in farm buildings that are surrounded by open fields and upland woods on Lawrence Hill Road, in Cold Spring Harbor (516) 367-3225. There are trails through the uplands here, and they have a detailed guide available.

We wrote briefly about the Nature Conservancy in Walk #8, East Hampton Beach. Though it is a national organization, it works quietly and most effectively on the local level, and the two chapters on Long Island have been responsible for the acquisition of more than seventy natural areas here, many of them ecologically fragile. The Sunken Forest on Fire Island, the North Shore Wildlife Sanctuary, and a section of Caumsett State Park are each properties that the Nature Conservancy helped to set aside for conservation purposes.

A number of these natural areas that belong to the conservancy we have walked with great satisfaction, and they are open to serious walkers with permits. If interested, you should contact them directly. With your help as a member even more can be accomplished.

We have hesitated to include the Manor of St. George amongst these walks because it is closed for much of the year. However, we do suggest you plan a visit to this William Floyd homestead, an old farm of the Colonial era at the eastern tip of Great South Bay in Mastic Beach, Suffolk County. It is now administered by the U.S. National Park Service, and there is no entrance fee.

This place is a great three-story house on a 127-acre site, with fields ending in the salt marshes of Bellport Bay. The mixture of woodlands and open fields makes for excellent walking; in addition, the peat bog and salt marsh are fine for birding. In fact, it is a bird sanctuary, and with the Wertheim National Wildlife Refuge just north along the Carmans River (which empties into Bellport Bay) and above that the Southaven County Park (busy in summer), there are substantial parcels of protected land surrounding it. These things and the setting, flowers, and fine old trees make for enjoyable exploring.

In 1693 the estate was granted to a British army colonel, William Smith, but later became the homestead of William Floyd. You can read about this and see documents on display as well as early-nineteenth-century paintings in a visit to the house. William Floyd was born in 1734 at Brookhaven to a family that had migrated from Wales. He had an unspectacular congressional career and was an officer in the Suffolk militia. A delegate to the Continental Congress of 1774 to 1777 and again in 1778 to 1783, he is remembered principally as a signer of the Declaration of Independence.

We suggest you check by phone (516–399–2030) for the opening or closing dates, which change, but the usual practice is to open the place in May and close in October. The hours are 10:00 A.M. to 5:00 P.M. Tuesday through Sunday. To reach it, turn at exit 58 off the Sunrise Highway or take exit 68 off the Long Island Expressway, head south on the William Floyd Parkway, then follow the signs just below Neighborhood Road in Mastic.

"We are not hikers—we aren't that goal-oriented," so say the Albrights, trying to make the distinction between walking to get somewhere and walking for fun. For them walking is to look and listen to all the sights and sounds of the woods, the meadows, and the sea.

Priscilla and Rod Albright lived in New York most of their adult lives, having come East to college and stayed right on. Rod was a television producer for a large advertising agency, and Priscilla served on the boards of several social service agencies.

Now retired, they do their daily walks from three different bases: in summer on an island in the Bay of Fundy where the craggy shores offer some scrambling and the woodland paths are full of birds and blueberries; in fall and spring they walk in the foothills of the White Mountains from a cottage in South Parsonsfield, Maine, near the New Hampshire border; come the depths of winter, a small Airstream trailer goes with them to Florida and Florida trails on pine needles or to the Southwest to walk in canyons or the floor of deserts because they are insatiably curious about the natural world.